THE ELEMENTS OF PSYCHOSYNTHESIS

Will Parfitt has twenty years practical experience with esoteric psychology, the Tree of Life and the Qabalah. He has trained in Psychosynthesis and has had extensive experience of other therapies and techniques for spiritual and personal development, including neo-Reichian therapy. He has a private psychotherapy practice and runs seminars and workshops around the country on a variety of topics. His work focuses on inner harmony and the manifestation of purpose and creative potential. When not working, Will loves to dance and is a keen photographer. His other books from Element include *The Living Qabalah*, *Walking Through Walls*, and *The Elements of the Qabalah*.

The *Elements of* is a series designed to present high quality introductions to a broad range of essential subjects.

The books are commissioned specifically from experts in their fields. They provide readable and often unique views of the various topics covered, and are therefore of interest both to those who have some knowledge of the subject, as well as to those who are approaching it for the first time.

Many of these concise yet comprehensive books have practical suggestions and exercises which allow personal experience as well as theoretical understanding, and offer a valuable source of information on many important themes.

In the same series

The Aborigine Tradition	Human Potential
Alchemy	The I Ching
The Arthurian Tradition	Islam
Astrology	Judaism
The Bahá'í Faith	Meditation
Buddhism	Mysticism
Celtic Christianity	Native American Traditions
The Celtic Tradition	Natural Magic
The Chakras	Numerology
Christian Symbolism	Pendulum Dowsing
Creation Myth	Prophecy
Dreamwork	The Qabalah
The Druid Tradition	Reincarnation
Earth Mysteries	The Runes
Egyptian Wisdom	Shamanism
Feng Shui	Sufism
Gnosticism	Tai Chi
The Goddess	Taoism
The Grail Tradition	The Tarot
Graphology	Visualisation
Handreading	World Religions
Herbalism	Yoga
Hinduism	Zen

> **the elements of**

psychosynthesis

will parfitt

Shaftesbury, Dorset • Boston, Massachusetts • Melbourne, Victoria

© Element Books Limited 1990
Text © Will Parfitt 1990

First published in the UK in 1990 by
Element Books Limited
Shaftesbury, Dorset SP7 8BP

Published in the USA in 1994 by
Element Books, Inc.
160 North Washington Street, Boston, MA 02114

Published in Australia in 1994 by
Element Books
and distributed by Penguin Australia Ltd
487 Maroondah Highway, Ringwood, Victoria 3134

Reprinted 1994
This edition 1997

Cover illustration by Martin Reiser
Cover design by Max Fairbrother
Typeset by Selectmove, London
Printed and bound in Great Britain by
Biddles Ltd, Guildford and King's Lynn

British Library Cataloguing in Publication Data
Parfitt, Will
The elements of psychosynthesis.
1. Self-realisation
I. Title
158.1

Library of Congress Cataloging in Publication
Data available

ISBN 1 85230 156 2

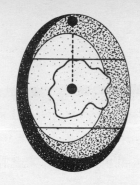

CONTENTS

Dedicated to
Joan Wenske
who guided me into psychosynthesis

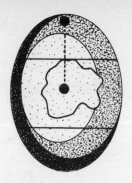

ACKNOWLEDGEMENTS

Eleanor Aitken, Malcolm Allum, Hannah Blacher, Gillian Broster, Carole Bruce, Rachael Clyne, Anita Courtman, Alan Dale, Dana Douglas, Hetty Einzig, Andrew Ferguson, David A. Findlay, Malli Gaster, Judy Fox Gray, Christoph Greatorex, Jean Hardy, Anita Harper, Susan Harrison, Nick Hedley, Helen Hennessy, Patti Howe, Lynne Hunter, Cecelia Jarvis, Graham Curtis Jenkins, David Jones, Tony Kennedy, Gabriel Knox, Anja Liengaard, Keld Liengaard, Alice Llewellyn, Dick Llewellyn, Gina Lomac, Douglas Mathers, Judith Meikle, Bob Miller, Jane O'Brien, Eve Parry, Cathy Pearman, Polly Plowman, Melanie Reinhart, Deike Rich, Ewa Robertson, Margi Robinson, Alison Sheriffs, Helen Sieroda, Keith Silvester, Brenda Squires, Barbara Thomson, Gayle Waleen, Barbara Ward, Jane Warman, Avril Wigham, John White, Neil White, Diana Whitmore, John Whitmore, and Ashen Venema for responding to the questionnaire which forms the basis of Appendix 1.

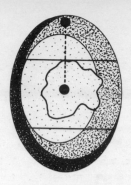

USING THIS BOOK

Each chapter of The Elements of Psychosynthesis is composed of two parts. First, there is the main text which introduces the subject of that chapter, and second there is an exercise, giving you the opportunity to try out psychosynthesis in an experiential way. The exercises are placed at the end of the chapter so that you can have greater choice as to how and when you practice them. You might like to do so immediately after reading the chapter, or you may prefer to leave them until you are feeling more in the mood. If you are reading this book whilst travelling, for example, you may prefer to wait until you get home before attempting an exercise.

Before starting any of the exercises, it is a good idea to spend a few moments relaxing and centring yourself. Ensure you have enough time to complete the exercise without being disturbed. Take up a comfortable position, either standing, sitting or lying as appropriate for the exercise, and with a straight but not stiff spine, close your eyes and take a few deep breaths. Be aware that you are a unique individual choosing at this time to perform this exercise. You are now ready to start the exercise. Take your time going through the instructions to the exercise – it is always better to err on the side of slowness rather than rushing through it.

It may be necessary to read the exercise through a few times to familiarise yourself with what you have to do. Doing this will help you focus on the exercise, so do not begrudge this time. If you find any particular exercise especially useful or meaningful to you, you can always repeat it more than once. Repetition of an exercise can, in fact, multiply its power in helping you realise more about yourself.

With some of the longer exercises, you might like to read the instructions slowly into a tape recorder, or get someone else to do this for you. You can then concentrate on the procedures involved without having to look constantly at the words. Alternatively, you might like to share the experience with someone else, each of you alternatively acting as guide and speaking the words and directions for the other person. If you do this, when you are acting as guide remember to respect the other person's process, and to speak slowly and distinctly, allowing him or her time to do whatever is required.

It is a good idea to keep a record of your experiences with exercises in a diary or workbook as, apart from anything else, it helps you ground the experience. This simply means finding ways of expressing what you've learnt in your everyday life. Mostly, however, have fun with the exercises – taking a light approach can help you connect with the work and keep a perspective on it.

Appendix 1 gives instances of how different people are applying psychosynthesis in their work. There are many ways to apply psychosynthesis and these 'user profiles' only describe some of these. Once you are using psychosynthesis in your life you will probably find many different ways you can effectively utilise it to enhance both your personal growth and self realisation. Appendix 2 gives suggestions about where to go if you are interested in learning more about psychosynthesis.

the strength and the power to express compassion according to wisdom; the wisdom and compassion to use power for the greatest good.

Roberto Assagioli

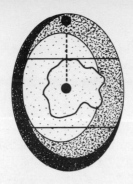

1 · WHAT IS PSYCHOSYNTHESIS?

Psychosynthesis is a method of psychological development and Self realization for those who refuse to remain the slaves of their own inner phantasms or of external influences, who refuse to submit passively to the play of psychological forces which is going on within them, and who are determined to become the master of their own lives.

Roberto Assagioli

Psychosynthesis is a comprehensive approach to self-realisation and the development of human potential. The essential aim of psychosynthesis is to help people discover their true spiritual nature, then to utilise this discovery effectively in everyday life. Psychosynthesis helps us to realise our creative potential, increase our ability to function harmoniously in the modern world, and improve the quality of all our relationships.

Psychosynthesis is a particular kind of psychotherapy, yet it is more than just psychotherapy. It is a collection of techniques and exercises designed to help us move away from what we don't want in our lives and towards what we do. It is not just a theory, but a practical, working method that integrates principles and techniques from many approaches to personal growth. Unlike some other therapies, however, it has no fixed idea of what someone 'should' be like – indeed, with

1

psychosynthesis, it is quite the contrary. It is only successful when we have become more what we wish to be like. This is not in the sense of gratifying unbalanced or partial desires, but when we have become more able to be ourselves in whatever situation we find ourselves, and to do what we want to do when we tune into our innermost sense of self and purpose. So psychosynthesis is a kind of therapy, and it is a method of self improvement, but more than this, it is also a process that co-operates with the unfolding evolution of all nature. It aims to bring awareness, wholeness and connection to the process of evolution happening in each of us.

Psychosynthesis has been described as 'a psychology with a soul', and this is what distinguishes it from many other forms of psychotherapy. Emphasising the value of intuition, inspiration and creative insight, it is a form of 'transpersonal psychology'. Whilst it concentrates on the personality, it also includes the realms usually ascribed to more mystical or esoteric doctrines. Yet, while it explores these areas that we could call spiritual, it in no way imposes any form of doctrine or belief system upon the person using it. Psychosynthesis is not a religion, nor would it ever want to be. Although once you start doing psychosynthesis it becomes a way of life, one of its greatest qualities is that it allows you to be and do whatever you want. So it is equally suitable for Christians, Buddhists, Pagans, Moslems, aetheists, agnostics – indeed, anyone at all.

Psychosynthesis is a way of understanding our lives, of helping us to know ourselves and trust in our own processes of growth and unfoldment. But psychosynthesis does not deal only with the individual, for each of us is part of many different groups of people, including our families, our friends, our work mates, and so on. We are also members of a society and of the one human family that covers the whole planet.

Psychosynthesis honours both the individual and the groups to which the individual belongs. Partly because of this inclusive attitude, and partly by the nature of its transpersonal connection, psychosynthesis is not a way of putting ourselves above or over anyone else. We can honour and utilise our own wishes and power but not at the expense of other people.

Psychosynthesis does not rigidly analyse or label people and it is expected that we will not do this either.

Many people in our modern world suffer from either one or both of two main crises. Firstly, there is the 'crisis of meaning'. Particularly in the western world but increasingly over the whole planet, many people live in an existential vacuum, where life has lost its meaning (beyond the purely material). Psychosynthesis helps with the healing of this 'illness'. The second crisis is that of 'duality' – we do not know ourselves as whole, single entities, but are constantly torn between different desires and wishes. Psychosynthesis works on the healing of this crisis through moving all our constituent parts towards a clearer harmony – synthesis in fact.

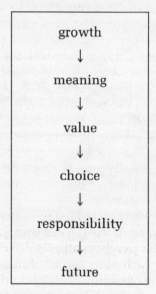

The Forward Path

Psychosynthesis recognises that each of us is constantly growing. This viewpoint helps to put meaning and value back into life, and helps us make decisions about who we are and what we want. It can also help us realise our re-sponsibility both to ourselves and the world as a whole. It can add a dynamic sense of self to the present moment, and a sense of meaning to ourselves and to our future.

Psychosynthesis can help you to 'know yourself' in the fullest sense of these words. In our modern world situation there is much strife between people on an individual and collective level. The poor ecological state of our world is due to the greed of some people and the mindlessness of others. There often seems to be an appalling lack of care and understanding and so much imbalance, particularly in the interaction between people. Anything which helps people know themselves better, both as individuals and in the context of living a life in accord with others, has to be useful.

To summarise, psychosynthesis offers:

- a means whereby we can grow and learn more about ourselves;
- more ability to do our will, to take actions that improve our situation both from an inner and outer viewpoint;
- a connection to the transpersonal realms of soul and spirit;
- a clearer connection to our conscious life processes and to the unconscious realms behind these;
- more creativity;
- a way of grounding creative energies and manifesting our true life purpose;
- an improvement to our inner life;
- better interpersonal relations.

BACKGROUND

Psychosynthesis was founded by an Italian called Roberto Assagioli (1888–1974) earlier this century. He had trained as a psychoanalyst but also had an interest in the esoteric. The more he worked with people in the analytical mode, the more he felt there was something missing, some vital aspect of the person that was not being honoured or addressed in any way. This was the transpersonal or spiritual realm which includes spiritual understanding, wisdom, love and inspiration. Assagioli once said that psychoanalysis was primarily concerned with the basement of the psyche whereas psychosynthesis is concerned with the whole building. Once we learn to access the whole building, it is then possible to include all aspects of ourselves. We can live in a more holistic way, including not only ourselves but, through the connections that are inevitably made once the spiritual realms are accessed, all other living beings.

The key to understanding the development of psycho-synthesis out of psychoanalysis can be found in the words themselves. *Analysis* is the separation of something into its component parts so that its nature and function can be understood. This, indeed, forms part of psychosynthesis. *Synthesis* goes further, however, by putting everything back together again, in a new way that synthesizes these component parts more harmoniously. They create a new unity, placed around a centre at the core of the being, from where the individual can more effectively direct his or her life. Synthesis actually means putting together the parts of something so as to form an integrated whole. All our parts – mental, emotional, physical and spiritual – have to be included for the synthesis to be effective and complete.

Modern psychologists, particularly those working with people in a practical way, whatever their discipline, take the role that was once ascribed to the 'wise person' or 'shaman' in the society. They are expected to have an understanding of the inner world and to be able to use this understanding to heal people. If we want to heal someone we have to 'make them whole' (the word 'heal' has a common root with the word 'whole'). Psychosynthesis, by including the spirit and soul, allows a thorough healing to take place. It also has a connection through this to esoteric traditions that are much older than modern psychology.

Since Assagioli's death in 1974, psychosynthesis has grown worldwide and there are now training centres in many countries in the world, and psychosynthesis practitioners in all walks of life. Psychosynthesis does not only teach you how to work with and 'heal' other people. Many people who train in psychosynthesis do just that, but the majority of people who undertake psychosynthesis – either as a training, with an individual guide or simply through using the techniques they learn from books – then utilise psychosynthesis in their own field of work. This includes education, medicine, social work, the arts, engineering – you name it and the principles of psychosynthesis can be applied to it. All the signs suggest that psychosynthesis is continuing to grow, for unlike some other similar methods for personal understanding, it is not a finished system but one that is willing to change and grow as the world changes and grows.

HARMONIOUS GROWTH

Psychosynthesis is not only a method for self realisation, but a continuous and organic process that is happening in the psyche of everyone at all times. This process happens naturally, but it tends to get blocked. The methods of psychosynthesis include techniques for unblocking this process. These techniques are not used mechanically, but are applied with care and attention. They can then act as transforming agents in our lives, and put us in touch with the natural flow of growth and development.

To help understand the process of psychosynthesis, it has been found useful to split it into two parts – 'personal' and 'transpersonal' (or 'spiritual') psychosynthesis.

Personal psychosynthesis concentrates on building a personality that is effective in the world and relatively free from blocks of any kind, able to direct its energies constructively, and that has a clear awareness of its own centre or 'I'. Each of us has a centre or 'self' which when contacted helps us organise, and ultimately synthesise, all the various parts of our being. To reach this centre we have to use our will. This will is not at all like the old fashioned concept of will-power – something that you have to struggle with in order to make things work – but is rather something fluid and easy, something which, as we approach our self or centre, we find becomes easier, and is even fun.

To really harmonise all the various parts of the individual it is essential to have this centre, called the 'I' in psychosynthesis, around which the synthesis can take place.

The more the sense of this 'I' is realised, and the more contact is made with it, the more we can then realise our even deeper connection with spiritual realms. In psychosynthesis this deeper centre is called the Self (with a capital 'S' to distinguish it from the self with a small 's' which is another name for the 'I'). When we succeed in unifying the different parts of ourselves, and move a little towards the Self, we experience the release of positive energies such as Joy, Truth, Happiness, and Unity.

The first stage of psychosynthesis is, therefore, analysis which helps the individual to get a thorough knowledge of the personality. Next comes the work of personal psychosynthesis, focusing on ways to control and integrate the various parts of the personality. This is based on the main principle of psychosynthesis which can be stated thus: '*We are dominated by everything with which we become identified or attached. We can dominate and control everything from which we dis-identify or dis-attach ourselves.*'

We can achieve this dis-identification through contacting our unique and unattached centre. When we feel the surge of an overwhelming wave of anger, for example, we no longer either need to suppress it or let it take us over and explode out in whatever form it chooses – both ways in which it has us rather than we have it. Instead, we can have the anger and find ways to express it appropriately, or we can discharge the energy in other ways (for example in creative acts) if the anger is inappropriate.

When you have it rather than it has you, the 'you' that has it can say 'I have anger' (or whatever it is). Who is this 'I' that has it? The 'I' that is your centre or self, the you that is pure self awareness, unattached to anything but willing to identify with the contents of your consciousness as appropriate. Once we have made good strong connections with this 'I', the next step of psychosynthesis is the reconstruction of the personality around this centre.

Transpersonal psychosynthesis explores the spiritual regions, areas beyond our ordinary awareness. It is in such areas that we find the source of all intuition and our sense of value and meaning in life. For many people personal psychosynthesis is enough, as it helps them become harmonious individuals, well adjusted within themselves and within the communities or groups to which they belong. However worthy an achievement this may be, however, for some people it is not enough and they touch on a real need inside to develop spiritually as well – this is when transpersonal psychosynthesis comes into its own.

Psychosynthesis includes the whole person, which is composed of the personality plus the spiritual realms, including the Self which is, in this sense, our connection to the divine (whether that is seen as some outside energy or ultimately within us). Using psychosynthesis we can learn to grow on all these levels. We can develop as a personality and find more effective ways to experience life and to express ourselves. We can also grow in our connection to the transpersonal realms, thus unleashing more positive, beneficial elements into our lives. We find more effective ways of utilising our creative energies. Creativity, in the psychosynthesis sense, is not just about drawing, painting, making music, sculpting or whatever (although it is these things as well), but acknowledges the fact that we are all creative in our own ways. With the right attitude we can be as equally creative doing housework as in painting a masterpiece, in changing a baby's nappy as in encouraging it to walk and talk.

Everything in nature appears to be evolving towards increased wholeness. This could even be considered to be the definition of evolution. An atom comes together with other atoms to form a molecule, and these form cells, which then group into tissues which become organs that make up a whole body. A similar process of synthesis can be seen in our psychological world, too, as all the parts of us come together to make us into one, whole person. We can use psychosynthesis to help us explore all these parts so we become more centred and able to function more effectively. If one molecule was at war with another, and your heart didn't agree with your lungs, you'd have problems. So it is with the psychological functions too – when our sensations, feelings, thoughts, emotions, imagination, intuition, everything that makes us up, are harmoniously synthesised, then we work well and without conflict.

Synthesis respects the individuality of each part. No bit of us is 'better' or 'worse' than another bit. On the contrary, psychosynthesis says that each part has to be whole before it can truly be synthesised and integrated. The conflicts we experience can be seen in this light – as the source of the energy which allows us to know more about ourselves. When we work on our inner conflicts, we can utilise the released energy to function more effectively. In other words, apparent obstacles can be seen as gifts which we can value as much as the more obvious gifts when things are going well.

We can know what we want, and have an idea of where we are going in life, but once we start moving in that direction we find there are all kinds of blocks that stop us. Psychosynthesis says that these blocks are our helpers. Through looking at them and dealing with them, we can move more effectively in the direction in which we desire to go. The blocks are the very energy of our being, so the more we deal with the blocks the more we are moving towards our true being, rather than cutting off from ourselves and not allowing our potential to grow and blossom.

Once we start making choices about where we are going or what we want in life, one of the first major obstacles we meet is all the conditioning we have received as children (and often are still receiving through advertising and political control). This conditioning is most clearly seen in the things we believe we 'should' do – should go to bed early, should wash your teeth, should be good girl and so on. We have to move towards a freedom of choice and not allow these 'shoulds' to control our actions. This is not always so easy. We think we 'should' do something even though it is not what we really want to do, so how do we do what we want to do without being in conflict with the part of us that says 'you should . . .'? One of the aims of psychosynthesis is to help us understand that we are always bigger than the dynamic of any such conflict – if we move out of the conflict and connect with the self, from this better vantage point we can make clearer decisions.

When we have peak experiences, times when we feel really connected and 'right', when everything around us feels harmonious, and our lives are filled with qualities such as Love, Joy, and Truth, we can make positive affirmations that will expand us and help us to include even more of these qualities. But we also have to find ways of manifesting or grounding these energies or they will dissipate into illusion. Psychosynthesis deals both with the connection to these qualities and the ways in which we can ground them. In psychosynthesis the work is never a process of 'getting rid of' something but is rather aimed at transformation through inclusion. Through honouring transpersonal qualities and getting more in touch with them, then expressing them clearly, we can bring more harmony to our personality. In other words, we are able to manifest more of our potential.

Although we can go to a psychosynthesis therapist (usually called a guide) for individual sessions, or to a psychosynthesis group either for training or group therapy, psychosynthesis is basically a system of self help. This is not to say that seeing a guide or going to a group does not enrich and often speed up the movement towards wholeness, but in psychosynthesis the aim is always to 'give the power' to the client. The ultimate aim of psychosynthesis, whether we learn about it through a book or go to a guide, is to enable us to do it for ourselves. Psychosynthesis does not promise any kind of standard result; how any individual's psychosynthesis unfolds depends upon that person alone. With practice, experience, intelligence and intuition, however, real and satisfactory results can be achieved.

OPENING EXERCISE – THE SYNTHESIS OF PARTS

Find a comfortable position, either sitting or lying down, in which you feel relaxed but alert. Take a few deep breaths and allow yourself to become as calm as possible.

Imagine a single atom. See the nucleus and the electrons spinning around it. Take some time to really imagine this atom in your mind's eye.

Now imagine this atom combines with another atom, then several more atoms until they form a molecule. Clearly imagine a molecule composed of several atoms.

Molecules can come together to form cells. Imagine you see this happen, imagine your molecule merging with other molecules and cells forming. Take some time to really imagine this process.

Every living thing on our planet is composed of such cells. Your body is made up from an innumerable number of cells that have formed themselves into tissues, organs, blood, bones – everything which makes you what you physically are.

Realise that you are made up from cells. Your unity is dependent upon the harmonious interaction between countless cells which are in turn dependent upon the synthesis of equally countless numbers of molecules and atoms.

On a physical level, all these parts come together to make up 'the whole you'. Allow yourself to really connect with how wonderful this is.

Realise the same is true for your inner world, too. All the parts of you – your thoughts, feelings, emotions, sensations – everything that constitutes you, is part of this one, whole being you call 'myself'. Allow yourself to really connect with how wonderful this is.

In your own time, bring your awareness back into your room and spend some time simply being with the thoughts, feelings or sensations you may be experiencing.

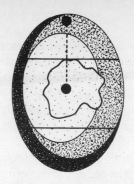

2 · THE
INNER JOURNEY

Spiritual development is a long and arduous journey, an adventure through strange lands full of surprises, difficulties and even dangers. It involves a drastic transmutation of the 'normal' elements of the personality, an awakening of potentialities hitherto dormant, a raising of consciousness to new realms, and a functioning along a new inner dimension.

Roberto Assagioli

When we are exploring ourselves and our relationship with other people and the world around us, it is very helpful if we have a map. There are lots of different maps of consciousness, some better than others. One of the best maps is the one used in psychosynthesis, sometimes called 'the egg of being' or quite simply 'the egg diagram'.

A good test of a map of consciousness is to see whether it becomes dated as new information about our human consciousness and how we operate comes to light. Just as if we were travelling in, say, Spain, we would fare much better if our map showed Spain as it is now, not as it was a hundred years ago. It is also important to choose a relevant map – a map of Italy would be of little use to us on our trip to Spain. Similarly, an out-of-date or irrelevant map of human consciousness will also be of little use to a modern day traveller.

A good map helps us to see where we are, and our relationship to both where we have come from (the past) and to where we are travelling (the future). It will help us to see who we are, particularly as it focuses us onto our present moment in both time and space. A good map should help us understand ourselves, both intrinsically and in relation to other people and things.

Good maps shouldn't really need too much data to be read properly, but all maps need some explanation. At the very least we need a guide to the symbols on the map. Without it how would we know that a little black circle with a cross above it is a church with a spire? A good guidebook will help us to read the map in the most effective way. It might tell us, for example, that the brown lines with numbers are contour lines, and that when they are close together the ground is steep, or when they are far apart it is flat. A good guidebook will also give us some information to help us really appreciate where we are, the 'local colour' of the place. It is the primary purpose of this chapter to act as a guidebook to the psychosynthesis map, 'the egg of being'.

It is of vital importance wherever we travel, inside or outside of our own consciousness, to be ourselves. But when we travel in unknown or new places, it is well worth remembering to proceed with caution, checking with our map and guidebook more frequently than we might once we are familiar with the territory. And, finally, it is of most importance to remember that if any particular map doesn't work for us, we are probably better off finding a different one that does. Psychosynthesis will work for us even if we don't really like or wish to use 'the egg of being' map. Indeed, psychosynthesis will work equally well with other maps such as, for example, 'the tree of life' which is the map used by Qabalists to experience and explore different states of consciousness.

Whether we choose to use another map or this one, it is always worth remembering and reminding ourselves that the map is most definitely not the territory. All maps are static versions of a dynamic reality. They are not the truth, but representations of it. They are, however, useful tools for facilitating our inner exploration.

13

When we get right down to it, and are actually exploring ourselves, we have to really experience the territory, to become fully involved in the experiences we are having. Thus it is well worth spending some time studying the map so that when we are actively travelling – climbing a psychological mountain, bridging an emotional river, descending into a well of spiritual understanding, whatever we are doing, we are helped by our familiarity with the territory.

The main psychosynthesis map, called 'the egg of being', represents our total psyche. The three horizontal divisions of the egg stand for our past (1), present (2) and future (3). All three are constantly active within us, although in different ways. This is obvious when we consider the present moment – after all, we are here and now not then and there! Within this present moment, this 'here and now', we carry the past with us in the form of all our memories and experiences whether we remember them or not. In one sense, it is everything from the past that makes us what we are in the present moment. In another sense, perhaps more 'esoteric' but no less real, we also carry the future within us. It has not happened yet, but all of us have right now the potential to become something else, to

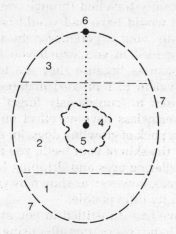

The Egg of Being

have new experiences, to find new ways to express ourselves. Or perhaps someone's potential might be to remain always the same, to experience or express nothing new – but that, too, is something they carry within themselves.

The egg of being is chiefly concerned with our inner journey and so its 'divisions' represent the different aspects of ourselves as individual beings, and our connection to other beings too. Study the map as you read the following descriptions so that, as your familiarity with the map increases, so does your familiarity with the different aspects of yourself.

(1) represents the *lower unconscious*, our personal psychological past which includes repressed complexes, long-forgotten memories, instincts and physical functions over which we (ordinarily) have no conscious control. All our fundamental drives and 'primitive urges' are part of this realm as are the activities of basic bodily functions. It is primarily the repressed material, often experienced in the form of unconscious controls upon us, phobias, obsessions, compulsive urges and so on, with which we are primarily concerned in psychosynthesis.

If you had recently travelled through, say, Turkey, all the experiences you would have had would have changed you, and would 'colour' your experience right now. Some things might have happened to you which you have pushed out of your consciousness because they are too unpleasant to remember (equivalent to repressed material). Although you might have chosen to 'consciously forget' these incidents, they would nevertheless have an effect on you. If you had been chased by a pack of growling dogs, for example, and you only escaped by the skin of your teeth, you might not want to remember their glaring eyes and dripping fangs. Their effect would still be there, however, as shown by your reaction right now to that friendly little poodle!

You might have had it instilled in you as a child that you must wash your hands every time after using the toilet. This in itself is sound advice, but you were conditioned into believing you have to do this or you are naughty. But here in 'Turkey' you cannot always do this and after every time you use the toilet you feel a little sick. Of course it may be that you are being affected by some bacterium. It could equally be that, although you have forgotten it, you are really being affected by the parental voice that somewhere in your unconscious still tells you off when you don't do what you are told.

These are just two examples of the many, many items that we carry within us in our 'lower unconscious' that may affect us at any moment. Watch out for other such examples but do not be surprised if you find this difficult – after all, part of the power of such incidents from the past is that they are no longer remembered and thus exert that much stronger a hold on us. Luckily for us we do not have to remember them as they are constantly emerging from the unconscious in various guises anyway.

When we explore our lower unconscious it helps our growth because as we learn to integrate more of these 'older' or repressed aspects of ourselves, the more whole we become. When we release previously repressed energies, we feel healthier, have more energy available to us, and feel more freedom in our lives.

(2) represents the *middle unconscious*, the place where all states of mind reside which can easily be brought into our *field of awareness* (4). For example, in our readily accessible 'middle unconscious', we carry all sorts of information and knowledge which is not always relevant. We know how to do simple arithmetic, but do we really want to choose to have that in our consciousness when we are making love? We know how to bake a cake but do we want to be thinking about that when we are reading these pages?

You might know that later tonight you have an important meeting with a friend, but you can safely let that knowledge reside in your middle unconscious until later. Of course, if it is a very exciting meeting, then all through the day it will keep popping into your mind, perhaps distracting you from whatever else you are doing.

The middle unconscious also holds suppressed material. This differs from repressed material which has been 'pushed down' into the lower unconscious. With repressed things we no longer 'remember' or own them as part of us. Suppressed material, on the other hand, we know is there, it is just that we are choosing, for one reason or another, not to bring it out at this moment. For example, you really want to eat something, but you have to suppress the desire until lunchtime when you are free to go to a cafe. Or you know something about a friend of yours but you are choosing to suppress this knowledge for fear of upsetting or hurting them.

There is nothing wrong with suppression, but we have to be careful that things that we suppress in our consciousness do not get completely forgotten, for they will then become part of the contents of our lower unconscious from where they will start controlling us rather than us controlling them.

The *field of awareness (or consciousness)* (4) is shaped like an amoeba to emphasise how it is constantly changing as our field of awareness changes. Often it is simply shown as a circle, but I prefer to shape it like an amoeba to emphasise how it constantly changes. The field of awareness is constantly alive with sensations, images, thoughts, emotions, feelings, desires and impulses all of which we can observe and act upon or not as we see fit. One moment you are relaxing with your lover, say, and have a 'pseudopod' (or arm) stretched out to your feelings. Then the phone rings, it is a call from your work and now you retract the pseudopod that was into feelings, and stretch yourself, as it were, into a mental place, where you can connect with the conversation about work.

Our field of awareness is constantly fluid, changing as our feelings or thoughts or sensations send us information about our environment. If we become really cut off from our experiences it can be as if the amoeba of awareness 'encysts', it hardens its semi-permeable skin and stops letting through clear messages, either from inside to outside or vice versa. Part of the work of psychosynthesis is to bring freedom of movement to our amoeba, and to increase our awareness of its function and abilities.

17

(3) represents the *superconscious*, our evolutionary future, the region from where we receive all inspiration and illumination, however we experience it. Indeed, true inspiration can come to us in artistic or scientific, very grand or very simple ways. It is the source of our 'inner genius' and is thus perhaps the major area of exploration for us when we wish to move into our future more clearly and successfully. We will be looking at the realm of the superconscious later in this book.

Perhaps the most obvious way that most people connect with their superconscious is through insights and 'inspirational flashes' that just seem to appear in their consciousness. For instance, you might suddenly realise the solution to a problem that has been bugging you for days. Or you might suddenly know more about what you want to do with your life after months of feeling uncertain and directionless. Usually such insights, and other similar 'relations', show that the superconscious has been contacted.

The exploration of these three realms, the lower, middle and higher unconscious, is one of the main tasks of psychosynthesis. Any distinction between higher (or super) unconscious and lower unconscious is developmental, not moralistic. The lower unconscious is not bad, or in some sense not as good or as important, it is simply earlier in our evolution. It is described as 'lower' simply because it is behind us, and forms the 'foundation' of our present awareness.

The superconscious is not merely an abstract possibility but a living reality with an existence of its own. Calling it superconscious (or 'higher' unconscious) does not mean it is above us or better than us in some way, it is merely meant to describe the sense that as we evolve it is as if we are raising our consciousness into new experiences. Alternatively, when insights come from this realm of the unconscious, we often get a sense of things 'dropping into place'.

(7) represents the *collective unconscious* that is common to all living beings. We are not isolated pieces of individuality, we are not islands, so although at times we may feel isolated and alone, in reality we are part of a collective field in which all other beings play a part. There is a constant and active interchange between us and all other sentient beings, whether we are aware of it or not.

Note how in the egg diagram the lines are dotted to show there are no rigid compartments impeding free interplay between all these 'levels'. If we become too rigid it is as if the egg 'hardens' and our work might be to crack it a little to let more fluidity into our lives. On the other hand, if we are too sloppy, too 'nice' for our own good, if we find it difficult to separate ourselves from other people, then it is as if the spaces in the egg have become too large, letting in (or out) too much. Our work is then to strengthen the egg shell, and create more of an individual identity.

(5) is the *personal self*, our individual 'I' who experiences all these different states of consciousness. It is the 'I' that experiences itself as having thoughts, emotions and sensations. It is not these changing contents of consciousness (thoughts, emotions, sensations, and so on) but the inner you that experiences these contents. Generally during life we do not experience this 'I' in a very clearly defined way. The more we work on ourselves through psychosynthesis, the more we can start contacting the 'I' and make it a living, experienced reality in our consciousness. In one sense we could say on both a psychological but also a physiological level, that the more we get in touch with our 'I' the healthier or more whole we become.

This personal self is a reflection or spark of the *spiritual or transpersonal Self* (6) which is both universal and individual. The realisation of this 'transpersonal' Self is a sign of spiritual success and achievement. Awareness of the personal self is the primary goal of psychosynthesis, for this is the place from where we can effectively direct the personality. This leads to a clearer and fuller contact with, and understanding of, the Spiritual Self.

THE INNER WORLD

Although it may seem obvious that the map is not the territory, in our lives we often confuse the two, and think that what we know about something is what it actually is. If we look into our inner world, using the egg diagram as a map, we find that all the divisions and so forth are very static representations of what is really an ever-changing, dynamic reality. But the map can help us to find our way round.

When we start investigating our inner world, we find that certain images and symbols seem easily to represent various aspects of ourselves. In psychosynthesis exercises, use is often made of the image of a meadow. This 'meadow', which you can visualise quite easily, corresponds roughly to the 'field of awareness'. Anything we then find in the meadow, or imagine to be there, is something within the contents of our middle unconscious.

We can imagine a track leading from the meadow down through some thick undergrowth into a mysterious, dark valley. This 'valley' can then represent our lower unconscious. We can also imagine a track leading up to a mountain on top of which we might imagine a Temple of the Self. This 'mountain' would then correspond to the superconscious. Of course, the mountain, the meadow, and the valley are not 'real' places, but how we imagine them, and what we imagine within them, are real representations of the inner world. In the following exercise, use is made of such imagery.

EXERCISE: VISITING THE MEADOW

Either lie down or sit in a comfortable position. Loosen any tight clothing you might be wearing, take a few deep breaths, then close your eyes.

Imagine you are in a meadow. Let your imagination really take you to a meadow on a summer's day ... Feel your feet on the grass. How long is it? ... Look around you −

what can you see? Are there birds, insects, trees? Really fill in as much detail as possible, and remember it is your meadow, there is no right or wrong way to imagine it.

Let your other senses come into play. What can you hear – perhaps the humming of insects, bird song, the sound of wind gently swaying distant trees ... What can you smell in your meadow on this warm summer's day? ... If you breathe in deeply, what can you taste? ... Take your time now to build the image of your meadow so that you feel really present in this place. Perhaps you might like to walk around a little, exploring the field. What are you wearing? What does it feel like to be in this meadow?

Be aware that at one edge of your meadow the ground gets rougher, and starts to slope away into what looks like a deep, dark valley. You can decide that perhaps one day you will explore that valley, but for now just be aware of its presence. How do you feel when you look towards that valley? What can you see in that direction?

Now turn around in your meadow and see that in another direction there is a path that leads up to a mountain. Really picture this mountain in all its splendour. Again decide that one day you will explore that mountain, but for now just be aware of its presence. How do you feel when you look towards the mountain? What can you see in that direction?

As you look towards the mountain, you see a bird flying towards you. See the bird getting bigger and bigger as it gets closer to you. In its beak it has a jewel and as it flies over you it drops this jewel and you catch it in your hands. Thank the bird for this gift, and sense the power and strength of this object as you hold it tightly in your hands.

Now look at the jewel. What does it look like – what colour is it, what size, do you know what kind of jewel it is? Get a clear picture of this jewel, then, when you feel ready, open your eyes, come back to your ordinary, everyday consciousness, and bring the jewel with you.

You might like to draw a picture of this jewel, or write about it in your diary or workbook. This jewel is a gift from your superconscious, and you can use it as a magical talisman which will protect you on your explorations into the depths – and heights – of your unconscious. Use it wisely and its strength and radiance will grow with you.

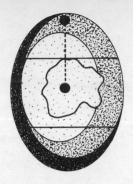

3 · THE MULTIPLE PERSONALITY

Psychological life can be regarded as a continual polarisation and tension between differing tendencies and functions, and as a continual effort, conscious or not, to establish equilibrium.

Roberto Assagioli

Life often seems to be an endless struggle between different parts of us wanting different things. The more we look at ourselves, the more it seems we are not whole, but composed of lots of different parts all having their own needs and desires. We are not split personalities, we are *multiple personalities*. Each of these 'little personalities' within us is called, in psychosynthesis, a subpersonality. Each subpersonality has a part to play in our lives and we all play many parts, often with conflicting thoughts and feelings about what is good for us, or even of who we actually are.

You might be a 'mother' seeing your children off to school, then the very next minute a 'housewife' washing the dishes. Later that morning you are a 'dancer' in your aerobics class, then a 'friend' for someone over lunch. Meanwhile your 'husband' has become a 'business man' in his office. Later tonight you will be alone together and become 'lovers'. This description may seem like a cliché, but often we live our lives in just such ways. All of us play such roles, often apparently flitting from one to another part with consummate ease.

How conscious are we of these parts that we play? Do you easily slip into a part of yourself that blushes and feels shy when in a crowd? Do you become an angry part of yourself just because you missed a bus? Are there times when you get 'stuck' as a housewife or a banker and wish things could change? Or perhaps you are so identified with a role you do not even realise it is a role you are playing. Instead you think it is the 'real' you.

Our personality is rather like an orchestra, and all these different parts or roles we play are like the musicians in that orchestra. As we become more able to define our lives, and control our processes in a positive inclusive way, we become like the conductor, allowing each individual member to play a part, and working towards orchestrating the personality into a harmonious whole. This conductor is the self or 'I'. As the conductor we will also contact the composer, the transpersonal Self, who will supply us with information about how to play the musical composition of life and also, perhaps, information about each individual player's part in the whole.

One way to start learning more about our different subpersonalities is to give them names. Roberto Assagioli suggested naming each of our subpersonalities with humour, both as a way of connecting to their energies but also to maintain a healthy detachment and lightness in this work. So, for example, a rather crazy emotional part of your personality could be called 'Loopy Len'; a bossy part 'Mrs Knowitall'; a rather dreamy little girl 'Alice' (in Wonderland); and so on. By giving our subpersonalities such names, we have identified them as not being all that we are, and have given them a 'handle' by which we can interact with them.

Spend some time now thinking about your different subpersonalities. It is a good idea to make a list of them, then see how many you can name. Thinking of your more prominent traits, attitudes and motives will help you start. For each part of you let an image emerge. It may be the image of a human of either sex, or an animal, a mythical creature, or anything at all. Do not 'make-up' these images for your subpersonalities, but rather let them spontaneously emerge from your unconscious.

You can start with the more obvious roles such as husband or wife, partner, daughter or son, businessperson, sportsperson and so on. Then consider subpersonalities that are based more around different states – the miserable old man, the angry cat, the fool, the controller, the top dog, the mystic, the sad little girl, the sensible adult, the shy boy, and so on. The aim is not to have the longest list of subpersonalities in town, but rather to know which subpersonalities you are aware of right now in your life. The list will change, and you can always add more subpersonalities as your work on yourself progresses.

When we first think of our subpersonalities, those we most easily connect with are part of what can be called our 'core personality'. These are subpersonalities we happily include as part of us. Some of these will be well integrated and be very helpful to us in our lives. They form the basis of what is sometimes called 'the ego'. They constitute who we believe we are.

Other subpersonalities are more suppressed. They are in the middle unconscious, we know they are there but we don't happily accept them as part of ourselves. Depending upon the

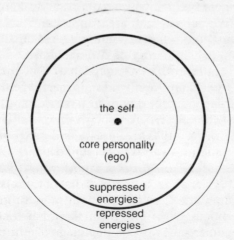

the self

core personality
(ego)

suppressed
energies

repressed
energies

The Personality

conditioning we have had, and various other developmental factors, they might include subpersonalities that represent 'forbidden sexual drives', parts of us that we hide away because we believe them unworthy, powerful parts of us that frighten our sense of who we are. They might also include self-assertive parts, which may become distorted into aggressive subpersonalities. They also include social conditioning, for instance, the 'top dog' who is always telling us what to do or not do.

For some people, almost everything they do is accompanied by the voice of an inner 'top dog' telling them whether it is 'right' or 'wrong', whether they should or should not be doing whatever it is. All of these suppressed subpersonalities are often projected onto other people. By this I mean that we often see in other people what is really in us. We may, for instance, accuse someone else of being angry, bossy, boring, or whatever, when in fact if we looked at our own state we could see it is us feeling these emotions. We may even project the feeling onto another group of people or the whole world in general. Think of the way immigrants are often blamed for a country's problems, or of the morose drunk who shouts: 'Sod off everyone and everything!'

Hidden deeper in the lower unconscious are repressed parts of us, primitive parts which are trapped and not accepted at all. They constitute what is sometimes called 'the shadow'. These parts of us can hardly be called subpersonalities as we know so little of them. They emerge and 'control' us at times, but generally we keep them well repressed. We have to learn to face these parts of us, so we can release the energy we are using to hold them down. When we release this energy, we usually find we have grown and transformed, perhaps only in a small or subtle way, but nevertheless in a very real and tangible way.

Psychosynthesis aims to expand our consciousness to include all three types. We can only transform subpersonalities when we connect with and fulfil their basic needs. Until then we remain fragmented. A fragmented personality might include a part that splits off, as if in trance, acting as if it is 'not at home'. Cut off from any true, direct experience, if it does express itself, it is often through pleading for its wants in a very unbalanced way. Or there may be parts of us that find their identity through others, always wanting more, never feeling as though they have had enough. A subpersonality like this only knows where it stands when in relation to someone (or something) else; otherwise it feels lost, and will generally do anything in its power to avoid these feelings of despair.

We can become so identified with some of the roles we play that it becomes very difficult to let go of them. Imagine a mother whose child has grown up and is ready to leave home. She loves this child and wants the best for him or her, but she is so attached to the role of mother that the separation makes her very sad. She is clinging to her role, and it is only through facing the sadness and accepting the loss that she will release enough energy to be able to move on. When she gets through this, and gives up her old role, she finds she has not 'lost' the child at all. And in no longer being so identified with the role she can, almost paradoxically, play it better.

Or imagine a man who has worked from nine until five in an office for most of his life. He has now retired and, sadly, he has been so identified with his role in his office, he doesn't know what to do with his new found time and 'freedom'. He feels bored, at a loss, and even catches himself wishing he could be back at the office. The retirement he has looked forward to no longer seems so attractive. He will have to find very definite ways to let go of his old role, and cultivate new interests to replace the old.

We all know people who, at least in some aspects of their lives, have not 'grown up'. For example, there might be a thirty year old man who still plays with his train set — perhaps when he does this he is really identified with one of his subpersonalities who is still a ten year old boy. Perhaps to avoid some of the painful issues he felt in adolescence he reverts, as it were, to an earlier time. Or imagine a fifty year old woman who still acts like an adolescent girl when men are around. We all have examples of such subpersonalities within us. It is as if all our 'little selves' are at different stages of development, some having reached full maturity, others at 'younger' stages,

27

even infantile when confronted with painful or difficult issues.

There is no suggestion that there is anything wrong with having subpersonalities. Far from it, they provide us with the means to interact with ourselves, other people and the world in general. Every subpersonality has an important part to play in our total being. Problems arise when they have got you rather than you have them. You come home after a day's work and you cannot stop thinking about it. Yet to 'dis-identify' from the role you might only need to take a bath and put on different clothes.

Psychosynthesis offers us techniques whereby we can discover the roles we play and then more clearly choose to either identify with them when appropriate and dis-identify from them when that is appropriate. This way our lives become more harmonious and we are more able to make choices about what we really want. Psychosynthesis, in other words, helps us to both become the conductor of our life orchestra, and also to play all the parts in the orchestra that we wish to play.

WANTING AND NEEDING

Our subpersonalities know what they want and are determined to get it. They really look out for themselves. This can be all right in itself, but problems arise when what one subpersonality wants is in conflict with the wants of another one. For instance, part of you might want to go to the cinema whilst a different part of you wants to stay at home. Perhaps one part of you might really need to leave a deadening job but another scared part won't let it happen.

Some of the deepest conflicts can arise between 'thinking identified' and 'emotionally identified' subpersonalities. You feel like telling someone you love them but you think they will laugh at you. Or you know it is a good idea to take regular exercise but part of you feels too lazy. Such inner conflicts can emerge in rather contradictory ways. A man might be a strong 'boss' at the office but at home a 'weak' husband and father. One day you might go out and be the 'life and soul' of a party, the next you are a mass of nerves, frightened of going out to the corner shop. The work in harmonising the relationship between the thinking and feeling functions can lead to the release of creative energy. This creative energy will be accompanied by the emergence of transpersonal *Qualities* such as Love, Joy, Truth and Beauty. We will talk of these Qualities in a later chapter.

To harmonise the wants of different subpersonalities, it is necessary to get behind them to the deeper level of needs. Needs are more inclusive than wants: 'I want you to hug me right now' and 'I want to respect your own choice' might be conflicting wants. When we contact the underlying need – perhaps 'needing more affection in life generally' – then we can find ways to fulfil this need without conflict. We can make this shift from 'wanting' to 'needing' through simply identifying the initial conflict then accepting it. We have to accept that if we cannot get away from it, we might as well include it. Once we are able to accept the wants of both sides of the conflict, a transformation is possible.

We need to get to know all our subpersonalities. We do this through dialoguing with them, letting them have a voice and realise their wants are being heard. Then we build a true relationship with them in which we attend to the larger needs of all concerned. We can learn to love all our subpersonalities in spite of their faults, and in doing this we give them the space they need in order to grow.

Many of the conflicts we see between different subpersonalities is an acting out of the dynamic between Love and Power (or Will). We can learn more about subpersonalities if we look at them in the light of this dynamic. Is a subpersonality content with simply being, does it want to be loved, or does it want to do, to act, perhaps to control? Does it feel most sad or hurt when it is not getting love or when it is not getting its own way? Is it angry because it feels there is not enough love in your life? Or is its anger a power issue?

The way to answer these questions is not by trying to work out the answers intellectually. Instead, you watch and observe your subpersonalities, hear what they have to say, and be aware of what they are feeling. Love-orientated subpersonalities tend to want to be included, listened to and taken care of. Power-orientated subpersonalities want to be able to express their needs, and not be restricted from taking the decisions they feel are right. Part of our work is to ensure these wants are met in harmonious ways.

Subpersonalities tend to be either ones who want everything (that affects them) to change, or ones who want everything to stay the same. These wishes usually interact in a dynamic way with the need for love or power. A love-type subpersonality, for instance, might want change: 'everything would be better if only you loved me'. Another love-type subpersonality might not want change: 'I couldn't live without you'. Psychosynthesis teaches us to co-operate with the process as much as possible – to choose change when that is most appropriate or to choose stability when that is the better choice.

To reach closer to the transpersonal Self, we have to learn to trust in both things that change and in things that stay the same, and at the same time not be attached to either. Awareness has to be coupled with psychological mastery. We can use our will power to stop us slipping mindlessly into different subpersonalities and be able to choose, at any moment, the most appropriate role to play. We have the ability to become the driver of our car, not just a back seat passenger.

The Qualities that emanate from transpersonal levels become 'degraded' in the personality: trust becomes foolishness, courage becomes foolhardiness, compassion self-pity and so on. Psychosynthesis helps us realise this, and it also helps us reverse the process. Qualities can also be 'elevated' in the personality – our self-pity becoming compassion and so on. The more we work in this way, the fewer problems of this kind we have in our daily lives. Although we might never reach complete unity, the more we move in that direction, the less distortions there are. If we could ever reach total unity in ourselves we would be free of all conflicts and distortions.

When we do any subpersonality work, however, it always releases energy and in so doing allows us to move closer to our centre and our true self. This expresses itself through the increased harmony we then find in our lives. Our multiple personality, our 'orchestra', as it grows and harmonises, becomes the ultimate healer of our divisions and fragmentation.

EXERCISE: THE GARDEN OF BEAUTY

In the next exercise you will meet a subpersonality who will take you into a beautiful garden. Enjoy the experience of this, and see how subpersonalities are not always in conflict, either with each other or with you.

Either sitting or lying down, take a few deep breaths and relax. Imagine you are in a meadow, and spend some time tuning into being there . . . What is the sky like? Is it a sunny day? . . . How do you feel? . . . What can you hear – bird song perhaps? . . . What can you smell? What do you see? . . . Be in your meadow as if it really exists.

In one direction you can see a small house or cottage. Walk towards it, feeling your feet on the ground, and remembering to pay attention to really being in your meadow . . . As you reach the house, you realise it is the home of some of your subpersonalities. You wonder who will live there, and how they will greet you. As you approach the door be aware of your excitement and anticipation.

You tap at the door and wait expectantly . . . Greet the person who opens the door to you, and pay attention to what he or she looks like. Is it a man, a woman or a child? Old or young? Fill in as much detail on this figure as you can . . . Then exchange some words, asking the person his or her name if you like. Find out as much as you are able about this person.

This figure then asks you into the garden. It is a beautiful garden filled with many different flowers, all radiantly blossoming in the bright sunlight. Pay attention to the flowers, their colours, scents, and absolute beauty . . . Allow yourself to be infused with the quality of these flowers . . . Walk with the subpersonality into the depths of the garden, then find one particular flower to which you are attracted.

Both you and the subpersonality look at this flower, brightly lit by a ray of sunshine. Feel the beauty of the flower transform your feelings and thoughts. Let yourself feel really good to be in this beautiful garden at this time.

Then turn to the subpersonality and see if she or he has changed. Engage him or her in dialogue and ask how he or she feels, what transformations, if any, may have taken place. Ask the subpersonality what she or he needs to maintain the beauty of this garden, and any changes there may have been.

Finally thank the subpersonality for taking you to the garden, say goodbye for now, and bring your consciousness back to your room.

Write about the experience, and the needs of the subpersonality, in your diary or workbook. In what way(s) can you express and fulfil these needs, or at least some aspects of them in your daily life?

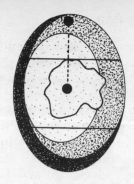

4 · SELF IDENTIFICATION

We are dominated by everything with which our self becomes identified. We can dominate and control everything from which we dis-identify ourselves.

Roberto Assagioli

In the last chapter we learnt about subpersonalities and how, although each subpersonality has an important part to play in our total being, problems arise when we become too identified or attached to any of them. It is as if they have us rather than us having them. There is the mother who is so identified with the role of being a mother that when her children leave home she cannot let go properly. The businessman who comes home from the office and is so identified with that role he cannot relax with his family but finds himself constantly worrying about what happened that day or what he has to do the next day. He isn't sitting there thinking, 'Oh I wish I could be less identified with this role I play at work.' On the contrary, more often that not he will be so caught up in the role no such considerations will arise. We can become so identified with a role that we never take the time to stop and see how we really feel. We might even believe we like being attached!

Another way of looking at how we become identified is through the functions we use to relate with the world – our bodies (and sensations), our feelings (and emotions) and our thoughts (or mind). Of course these three functions are not really that separate and are truly interrelated. If we look for example at our thoughts, then feelings and sensations will be there too. But it is useful to view them separately, both to help us understand them and to help us separate ourselves from them.

In our early years, from our birth maybe until around seven years of age, our primary focus for development is on our bodies. We are concerned with survival in our 'physical reality'. There is then a shift to development of our feeling function which lasts up to and through puberty. The emergence of sexuality can be seen as a joining of body and feelings. During our teens we are primarily concerned with the development of our minds and we often go through identity struggles involving the mind, feelings and body. Our development can be compared, as the diagram shows, to that of a three-leaved plant. The flower at the top then relates to the 'I' or self, which emerges into the light and draws energy from the transpersonal Self, represented by the sun in our diagram. To function most effectively, we need to have the whole plant available to us, all well developed and not lopsided, otherwise we will not be able to channel so effectively the rays from the sun (the Self).

To develop our personalities most effectively, we need a good connection with our bodies, feelings and mind. This connection can be best made through differentiation, which quite simply means we have to be able to tell, whatever is happening to us, whether it is truly an experience of sensing (body), feeling, or thinking (the mind). We can then get a better picture of which of these functions we use more and which tend to be overlooked in our everyday life. It will change for different situations, of course, but we can discover whether we are more mentally, emotionally or physically identified.

In psychosynthesis we try to raise the energy of the less well developed parts, mainly through inclusion. We also work on bringing more balance to the more suppressed functions. It

The Function Flower

is a principle of synthesis that each function must be made whole before it can be synthesised with other functions and fully brought into an integrated personality.

If you feel you need to develop a more balanced relationship with your emotions, for example, is it appropriate for you to go to that wild party tonight? Depending upon your individual circumstances it may be beneficial or not for you. But through bringing such awareness to play, and differentiating in this way, you can make clearer decisions rather than just following whims which might lead you off your chosen path of self discovery.

Another example might be found in a person who feels she wants to develop her mental function but finds it hard to read anything but monthly fashion magazines. Whilst there is nothing wrong with this in itself, that person might do far better choosing to read more mentally stimulating material. Alternatively, mental skills could be applied to the reading of the magazines – analysing their contents, looking at what is really being 'sold' in the pages between the ads, and so on. Part of the skill in working on developing and balancing our minds, feelings and bodies is in finding ways we can adapt the current situation, whatever it is, to our advantage in this way. How can we use our setting to aid rather than hinder our development?

It is important that we look at the relationship between sensing, feeling and thinking, asking ourselves how well do they work together in our personality? Then when problems arise, we can see them as opportunities to find out more about what is happening underneath, what is behind the problem. This gives us the opportunity to work on this deeper level. And, it must be stressed, in psychosynthesis we never wish to bring any function down to the level of a lesser function. Instead, we always work to elevate a weaker function so that it rises up to the level of a stronger one. If you are strong in feeling and weaker in thinking, then the work will be to develop the thinking function so that it is raised to the level of the feeling function. The work on the stronger function will be that of refinement. We cannot have a truly whole sense of who we are unless we are totally there!

Most people tend to be generally more attached to either their thoughts or their emotions, and can thus be described as mentally or emotionally identified. Such identification is useful for it allows us to inter-relate to the world around us. People who are predominantly identified with their thoughts, who are, in other words, mentally-identified, need to increase their awareness, experience and expression of their feelings, rather than diminish or decrease their mental awareness. This is balance through upward growth and inclusion, rather than through decrease and exclusion which is both unnecessary and inefficient.

Psychosynthesis uses various techniques to help us get to this deeper level of understanding. One of these techniques is 'time sharing', which means giving all the functions space for expression in our daily lives. If we give an angry, emotional part of us space for expression, for instance, it will then not come up inappropriately at other times, but will more readily 'time share' with other parts of our personality.

Another useful technique we mentioned in the last chapter is 'dialoguing', which means allowing different functions to communicate with one another to see what each has to say, both in terms of what they need but also what they can give.

Whenever there is a conflict, we can discover what is needed through listening to the voice of all the parts involved.

DIS-IDENTIFICATION

The experience of self-identification, of having an 'I', distinguishes our consciousness from that of the majority of other living beings on our planet. As far as we can tell, other creatures do not have a sense of self-consciousness. No dog seems to think: 'I am me, myself, separate and different from everything and everyone else'. We do not usually experience self-consciousness, in this way, either. It is usually experienced, not as pure self-consciousness, but rather mixed with and veiled by the *contents* of consciousness, that is, everything we are sensing, feeling and thinking at any time.

In psychosynthesis, we primarily see this separate unique self as the simplest part or 'unit' of our total being. It is our core. The self, seen in this way, is completely separate from everything else that constitutes our being – our bodies, feelings, thoughts, desires, all our subpersonalities, the different roles we play and so on. As it is separate, it is a place of unity and individual wholeness from where we can utilise and direct all these other elements that make us what we are in totality. And unlike these contents of our being, the self never changes, but remains the one static, unchanging, ever-present part of ourselves. One minute I am a father, then a lover, now I am feeling, then thinking – but I am always my self.

The self is what makes us who we really are, separate not only from all the contents of our consciousness, but also from everyone and everything else too. As selves we each have our own individual experience. Of course, someone might be identified and see herself as, say, a sportswoman. She might then become so identified with this role that she believes it is who she really is, rather than a role she is playing. Someone might become so identified with his feelings he loses sight of the rest of his functions. Thus the great value of being able to dis-identify from all these functions and roles and get to the true central core self. This self is not attached to anything, but is uniquely whole and centred in itself. From this place if you ask yourself: 'who am I?' the answer is not a sportsman, a mother, a banker, an angry person, a thinker, a fool, an actor, or anything other than 'I am me'.

Being identified is a bit like being in a dream where we move from one identification to another without awareness. Some Eastern philosophies compare our waking 'reality' to just such a dream. We don't realise we have, say, a particular feeling, we become the feeling. I don't have sadness, I become sadness. Such identification and attachment limits our perceptions. If we can awaken from this limiting dream, and identify with the self, we can come alive with a new awareness.

We are usually attached to or *identified with* the contents of our consciousness. To make self-consciousness an explicit, experiential fact in our lives, we need first to dis-identify from everything that fills us up and creates the contents of our consciousness. We have to become truly empty – then we find there is something left, this sense of 'I'-ness, of being a self, or simply being. Through deliberate dis-identification from the personality and identification with the self, we gain freedom, and the power to choose either identification with or dis-identification from any aspect of our personality, according to what is most appropriate for any given situation. Thus we may learn to master and utilise our whole personality in an inclusive and harmonious synthesis.

We often find it most difficult to dis-identify from our thoughts. We construct our world through our thoughts about it, so it can feel dangerous or difficult to stop thinking. Maybe our world will fall apart and we will be left in an unstructured, undifferentiated state. In actuality, however, we find we are left with the self, and have a new clarity in our lives we never knew could exist before. Indeed, when we stop our inner dialogue with ourselves, we find that special and extraordinary aspects of ourselves are able to surface. We can make more creative choices about our lives, and more easily find ways to manifest these choices.

When we dis-identify, we can then choose to re-identify. That is the goal. We don't want to be without our vehicles for expression and experience, we want to have them rather than them having us. It is as if when we re-identify with thoughts, feelings or the body, we can take a little bit of our new self-awareness with us. Not only have we found our 'I', the self, and are more able to dis-attach ourselves from the contents of our consciousness, but also we can more effectively control our being and doing in the world in a positive, life-enhancing way.

From this new perspective, we can truly say 'I am simply myself, and I have a body, and feelings and thoughts in order to experience the world and express myself in it.' With this new strength we usually find we are generally happier and more effective in our relationships with other people. On top of this, we also then have a 'safe anchor', so to speak, which allows us to explore more easily our lower unconscious and sort out some of the blocks, complexes, obsessions and other life-diminishing facets of our being. We have also, through this work, created more space for the influx of transpersonal energies into our personality. We are more able to manifest Qualities such as Beauty, Trust, Joy, and Truth.

The benefits of dis-identification, then identification with the self, cannot be over-stressed. You have already learned in the last chapter what is perhaps one of the simplest ways to start dis-identifying from various roles. Through recognising subpersonalities, and naming them, you are separating yourself from these roles. If you can see, for instance, that part of you is, say, 'a daughter', then you can realise you are not just a daughter. This applies to all our subpersonalities, whatever roles we play.

It is perhaps more difficult to directly dis-identify from the functions of thinking, feeling and sensing, but it can be done. It is achieved chiefly through a form of introspection whereby we become the 'observer' of our life. We can look at everything that happens to us as distinct from ourselves. If we are angry, for example, we can step back, become an observer, and see our anger. Then we realise we are not our anger, rather anger is something we have. We awaken from the dream, and see ourselves from a place of greater perspective. We might find it is right to be angry in the present circumstances, or not, but whichever is the case, we will have it rather than it having us.

The most important self-identification work we can do is through life situations as just described, when we observe ourselves from a separate place. As we do this more, we start to realise the self as a continuous truth behind all that happens in our lives. But it is always useful to forge links and strengthen our connection to the self, to help foster this natural process. The exercise which follows is the most important one in this book, and is central to the work of psychosynthesis.

EXERCISE: SELF-IDENTIFICATION

The following exercise is a tool for moving towards and realising the consciousness of the self. This exercise, called 'self identification' should be done with the greatest care. If you feel at all tired do not read on from here until you have at least taken a break. You will enjoy this exercise more if you are fresh when you first try it out.

Relax yourself in the best way you know how, putting yourself in a comfortable but alert position. Take a few deep breaths, and let go of any tensions from the day.

Follow these instructions slowly and carefully.

Affirm to yourself the following:

'I have a body but I am not my body. My body may find itself in different conditions of health or sickness, it may be rested or tired, but that has nothing to do with my self, my real I. I value my body as my precious instrument of experience and action in the world, but it is only an instrument. I treat it well, I seek to keep it in good health, but it is not myself. *I have a body, and I am more than my body.*'

Close your eyes, recall what this affirmation says, then focus your attention on the central concept: 'I have a body and I am more than my body.'

Attempt to realise this as an experienced fact in your consciousness.

Now affirm to yourself:

'I have feelings, and I am more than my feelings. My feelings and emotions are diversified, changing, sometimes contradictory.

They may swing from love to hatred, from calm to anger, from joy to sorrow, and yet my essence – my true nature – does not change. I remain. Though a wave of anger may temporarily submerge me, I know that in time it will pass; therefore I am not this anger. Since I can observe and understand my feelings, and can gradually learn to direct, utilise, and integrate them harmoniously, it is clear that they are not my self. *I have feelings, and I am more than my feelings.'*

Close your eyes, recall what this affirmation says, then focus your attention on the central concept: 'I have feelings and I am more than my feelings.'

Attempt to realise this as an experienced fact in your consciousness.

Now affirm to yourself:

'I have a mind and I am more than my mind. My mind is a valuable tool of discovery and expression, but it is not the essence of my being. Its contents are constantly changing as it embraces new ideas, knowledge and experience, and makes new connections. Sometimes my thoughts seem to be independent of me and if I try to control them they seem to refuse to obey me. Therefore my thoughts cannot be me, my self. My mind is an organ of knowledge in regard to both the outer and inner worlds, but it is not my self. *I have a mind, and I am more than my mind.'*

Close your eyes, recall what this affirmation says, then focus your attention on the central concept: 'I have a mind and I am more than my mind.'

Attempt to realise this as an experienced fact in your consciousness.

Next comes the phase of identification. Affirm clearly and slowly to yourself:

'After this dis-identification of my self, the 'I', from my body, my feelings, and my mind, I recognise and affirm that I am a centre of pure self consciousness. I am a centre of will, capable of observing, directing and using all my psychological processes and my physical body.'

Focus your attention on the central realisation:

41

'*I am a centre of pure self-consciousness and of will.*'

Realise this as an *experienced* fact in your awareness.

When you have practised this exercise a few times, you can use it in a much shorter form. The important point is to keep to the four main, central affirmations:

- I have a body and sensations, and I am more than my body and sensations.
- I have feelings and emotions, and I am more than my feelings and emotions.
- I have a mind and thoughts, and I am more than my mind and thoughts.
- I am I, a centre of pure self-consciousness and of will.

You may have to repeat the exercise a few times to start with to get its full flavour, but then you will be able to do it daily from memory. The effort will be well worth it. All the influences which try to capture your attention and demand identification will no longer have the same hold over you.

This exercise is effective if practised daily, preferably during the first few hours of the day. It can then be considered as a second, symbolic re-awakening.

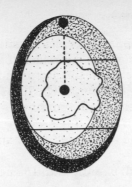

5 · SPIRITUAL GROWTH AND MEDITATION

Everything is spiritual that relates to the unfoldment or true progression of humanity . . . The hidden world is becoming as real to us all that we see, and we are beginning to awaken to the reality of a great Life in which we live.

Roberto Assagioli

It is possible for us to connect with the transpersonal or spiritual realms of energy. Meditation is one of the many ways to do this and we will be looking at it in detail later in this chapter. Other ways include dance, devotion, concentration, loving sex, aesthetic ecstasy, compassion, and shock. There are also many techniques and exercises which have been devised to help us connect with the spiritual, and psychosynthesis uses many of these.

As well as connecting with these spiritual energies, we can also manifest them in the world. It could be argued there is little point in us getting into contact with the spiritual unless we are going to utilise its transforming qualities in ourselves and our world. Psychosynthesis emphasizes this need for the grounding or manifestation of transpersonal energies.

A spiritual treasure, whatever form it takes, is only truly meaningful when it is 'brought back to the world'. The rich jewel that an explorer finds is of no value unless he brings it home and shares its splendour with others.

Of course, sometimes just connecting with the transpersonal realms can be enough. We might, for example, feel low and purposeless in our lives, then through a spiritual connection we might find there is hope and meaning after all. Or it might just be enough to know something more than mundane reality exists. But even if the spiritual connections we make only transform something inside us, it is still true that these energies will bring better human relations into manifestation. It is inevitable that if we, as individuals, transform ourselves in some way, that transformation will affect those with whom we come into contact.

When we connect with and manifest the transpersonal, we are more able to do our 'true will', to make our lives more purposeful. The 'higher' Self becomes more manifest through us, so we are truly co-operating with evolution. Then our own psychosynthesis can happen more readily, for we are aligned with rather than fighting against nature. And, in a truly dynamic sense, we find our everyday lives are improved. We feel more whole, more meaningful, happier, and those around us can share in this connection.

Sometimes transpersonal or spiritual energies 'burst in upon us' in a totally spontaneous way. As well as helping us make more connection with the transpersonal, psychosynthesis aims to help us deal with what happens when spiritual energy emerges more spontaneously. When energy comes upon us unexpectedly, it can be a very positive experience. We may either experience transformative 'highs' or quite simply feel a silent 'grace' pervading our lives. Sometimes, however, when such energies emerge unexpectedly, it is as if they are too much for the personality to cope with and we are 'blown out'. If we are fairly well prepared we can withstand these blow-outs and find ways of utilising the energy. If we are not prepared, then such energies can lead to all sorts of strange distortions of attitude and behaviour. We might think we are literally 'god', we might believe we are 'chosen' in some way, or we might become inflated in our sense of self. In extreme cases, this can even lead to dangerous behaviour both to ourselves and to others. Some psychopathic murderers say they have been 'spoken to' in some way. Perhaps in some cases the initial contact was genuine enough, but the personality was not able to cope with the energy and consequently it was channelled into a distorted message. Because of this danger, even if only manifested in a mild and fairly harmless way as is usually the case, psychosynthesis emphasizes work on the personality. The clearer we become in our personalities, the more able we are to deal with and constructively utilise our emerging transpersonal energies, whether chosen or spontaneous.

WAYS OF CONTACTING SPIRIT

Once we realise the great benefits to ourselves and our world when we contact the transpersonal realms, we want to know how we can do it more often and more effectively. From the many ways available, it is always best to find those that are appropriate for the person involved – 'different strokes for different folks' (or 'different scenes for different genes'!)

In the last chapter, we learned about the importance of Self Identification, and the exercise offered a good way of dis-identifying from the personality and identifying with the self. This technique is one of the most effective ways of connecting with the spiritual. In the first instance, by 'dis-attaching' in this way, we are bringing ourselves to our centre which in itself opens us up to such energy. Then we are also 'calling in' or 'invoking' the self, our distinct and unique 'I'. When we move closer to becoming 'a centre of pure self awareness and of will' then we are moving more into the spiritual realms and are thus more able to channel this energy into our personality and, through us, into our world.

It is very important to distinguish the Self from the super-conscious. The superconscious is a section of the whole unconscious and is, in fact, a rather artificial division. Our experience tells us that in reality the unconscious is not divided into sections. But for convenience it is most useful to make the three distinctions as shown on the psychosynthesis map. The 'superconscious' (or 'higher unconscious') is a description for that part of the unconscious that 'contains' energies of a higher frequency than those of the contents of the lower unconscious. This is not saying that one is 'better' than the other, but merely making a distinction to aid understanding.

The Self, on the other hand, is the central reality of a being, the innermost centre where he or she is completely individual and at the same time connected to everyone and everything else. The experience of this spiritual Self gives a sense of freedom and expansion to the individual. To experience the Self is of great value for it brings connection, revelation and spiritual maturity.

The Self never changes in essence, it is 'that which remains when all else is gone'. The superconscious is constantly changing, however, both as the Self radiates energy into it and then, in turn, it radiates energy into the personality. If we say the Self is like the sun, then the superconscious is the sun's rays, flowing to earth and giving life. We may each have our own individual experience of the sun, but in reality it is one sun that illuminates us all.

The Self is constantly radiating Qualities into the super-conscious. These 'Soul Qualities' include: Love, Truth, Beauty, Joy, Courage, Trust, Ecstasy, Delight, Unity, Calm, Compassion, Peace, Loyalty, Freedom, Risk, Power, Simplicity, Vitality, Understanding, Humour, Patience, Service, Wonder, Eternity, Vitality, and so on. In the superconscious all these Qualities remain in their 'pure form', undistorted in any way. As they come through to the middle unconscious and the personality they become distorted.

In psychosynthesis, when we talk about the 'distortion' of Qualities, we do not meant they 'go wrong' or are 'bad' in any way. It is simply that, in our usual personality state we do not either experience or express these Qualities in a pure form. How often have you given or received totally unadulterated, pure Love or Trust? We might be close to the pure experience, but there will still be something else operating at the same time. If a Quality becomes even more 'distorted' it can take on a 'negative' form. Love can become possessiveness, or jealousy, for example, or Trust might become fear or slavery.

At first sight, we might think that the distortion of Qualities in this way is a very negative experience. On the contrary, however, psychosynthesis teaches us that it is, in fact, very positive. If we can face our possessiveness, for instance, and deal with it appropriately, then it will transform into its underlying Quality. At the very least, some of the transforming energies of that Quality will be made manifest.

Someone might, for example, have a very devious sub-personality. Through subpersonality work, dis-identification and various other psychosynthesis techniques, this angry subpersonality might grow a little and feel that its needs are being better met. Then there is space for the emergence of the underlying Quality, which in our example might be 'Truth'. With the emergence of this Truth, a transformation can take place and the subpersonality – and through it, the whole person – can grow even more. Work on the psychosynthesis of the personality is thus a natural, on-going spiral of increase once the process is truly and clearly set in motion. Luckily for us, however, we never come to the end of this work – luckily because this means we have an endless reservoir of material we can transform. It is this process which allows us to ground or manifest our true creative Spirit, the Self.

GROUNDING

If we attempt to manifest any transpersonal energy or Quality into the world, it is ineffective so long as it is not grounded through the personality. Nothing can happen without a connection to ground. We have to connect clearly with our transpersonal energies and find ways to bring them effectively into the world. However bright or illuminating our insights and realisation might be, if the light is not radiated then it cannot help light our path let alone anyone else's.

If we can understand the difference between motivation and intention we can learn to ground our energies much more effectively. Intention essentially comes from a connection to the Self. Motivations, on the other hand, come from our responses to the outside world, and are 'chosen' by subpersonalities. Motivation and intention can actually be the same thing, or at very least be closely connected, but usually they are not.

Motivations are usually exclusive and are what push us into partial, uncentred and often ill-considered decisions and actions. They are a response, and often a victim kind of response at that. Intentions, on the other hand, are more about getting our deeper needs fulfilled. These needs are not so exclusive and are more about manifesting our Self and our True Will or Purpose. If I am motivated to want a banana then nothing else will do. I will get angry or upset if I don't get it. If I can contact my inner need more clearly I might find it is actually for fruit. I can now happily eat an orange and fulfil my purpose.

Whether we are dealing with the deepest intention of the Self or a simple desire or motivation from a subpersonality, we need a definite plan to fulfil it. This plan will tell us how we can go about manifesting or grounding our desire. This plan might include a need for us to be strong willed or we might just have to let go and accept what is. We might need to be single-minded, or we might need to deal with some emotional state before it can happen. Once we have done the preparatory work we are then able to ground our transpersonal energies.

There are several easy ways to ground energy, which include:

- simply expressing the experience;
- writing, and/or drawing;
- evening reviews (going over the past day and looking at how you performed, not as a judgmental exercise but in order that you might function more effectively through knowledge of how you habitually perform);
- meditation, either on the object of the will itself or a symbol you have constructed to represent the will;
- evocative word cards; sometimes called 'self-advertising' – you write your desire (in words or symbols) on postcards and stick them up around your home in places where you will frequently see them – just as with commercial

advertising, constant exposure has an effect on the unconscious;
- free or automatic drawing;
- creating a mantra and constantly chanting or repeating it to yourself;
- specific acts in your life, for example going to beautiful places;
- finding an object to represent what happened.

The most effective ways of grounding energy come from your own life situations. If you have never gone fishing there's little point (in the short term anyway) of grounding a need for fish though fishing. You'd do better to fit the need into your life situation and experience, that is, go to the local fish mongers!

Fear is a major block to grounding – it may manifest as fear of responsibility, of losing individuality, of impotence, of being a victim, of disrupting your life, of loneliness, of inadequacy, of being rejected, or even as the fear of success itself! Whatever gets in the way of our ability to manifest whatever it is we wish to do, the best way of dealing with it is to connect with who we are through Self-Identification. At the same time, we have to be willing to work through the blocks to our success with psychosynthesis and other similar techniques. Meditation can be particularly useful in that it helps us concentrate, connects us with our spiritual essence, and aids us in finding ways of expressing our inner truths.

MEDITATION

Many different meanings are given for the word meditation, and there are many different types of meditation and meditative techniques. At the simplest level, if we concentrate on something – anything at all – we are meditating. The more we discipline our thoughts, feelings and sensations to not intrude upon this concentration, the more deeply we can enter the meditative state. Many spiritual disciplines consider this work to be of prime importance.

It is often imagined that meditation is primarily an abstract activity, involved with turning inwards and somehow transcending the 'ordinary world'. In fact, meditation does involve concentration, reflection, understanding, being receptive and so on. It also includes, however, ways of bringing these connections into outer expression and it is thus also a very active and outer–directed technique. Meditation could be defined as the conscious and deliberate use of inner powers and energies to fulfil a specific purpose.

As a prerequisite to most types of meditation is to be able to still ourselves, the first action in meditation is to perform some acts that achieve this. We might slow our breathing down, sit in a particular posture, visualise a calming scene and so on. We have to shift our attention from its normal outward orientation towards the stillness of our inner world. To do this effectively, we can relax physically, enter a state of emotional peace and direct our thoughts to either stop or be one-pointed. Luckily for us, however, it is possible to meditate without achieving complete success in these preliminaries. The 'secret' is to centre ourselves as best we can (perhaps through the 'Self Identification' exercise), and then simply trust that the wisdom of the Self will lead us towards that with which we need to connect.

Psychosynthesis uses a form of meditation called receptive meditation. To truly be able to receive, however, we need firstly to clear our minds of all our thoughts about whatever it is we wish to meditate upon. This is done in psychosynthesis through a process called reflective meditation which, therefore, usually precedes receptive meditation. There would seem to be little point in connecting with the spiritual if we do not bring our new energy, connection and insights back to the mundane, material world. To find ways to achieve this, psychosynthesis uses a technique called creative meditation.

At times, of course, psychosynthesis uses many different forms of meditation, including contemplation, silent meditation, active meditation, one-pointed focusing and so on. But when we think of meditation and psychosynthesis, this threefold type of meditation – reflective, receptive and creative – usually springs to mind.

Reflective, receptive and creative meditation allows, if done in its entirety, for many levels of our being to operate and be active in our meditation. Each of these three 'types' of meditation can be done singly and often it is appropriate to do just that. If we combine the three together, however, it gives us the opportunity to meditate in a very thorough way that not only connects us to our inner being but also helps us express that connection. Both reflective and receptive meditation help us increase our spiritual awareness and thus deepen our ability to serve both ourselves and our fellow human beings. Indeed, all meditation is a form of service for as we make inner connections and express them outwardly we increase the overall level of awareness in the collective consciousness of the human race.

The following exercise shows you how to do all three and to connect them together, grounding the resulting insights. It can be adapted easily to any subjects upon which you wish to meditate, or adapted to create different methods of meditation.

MEDITATION EXERCISE

The first requirement for meditation, as for most of the exercises in this book, is to be able to relax. The most effective way is to find your own methods of relaxing and centring yourself. You might like to choose as quiet a place as possible. Choose a sitting position, either on the floor or in a chair, where you are upright but not rigid, your spine erect but not forced upright, and with your feet flat on the floor. You might like to have your hands loosely clasped in your lap and close your eyes. Before starting the meditative process take a few deep breaths and consciously choose to quieten your whole body. Through centring yourself, eliminate as much as possible from your consciousness (all thoughts, emotions, desires, plans, fantasies and so on).

REFLECTIVE MEDITATION

Reflective meditation could be called 'directed thinking'. For this exercise we will use the subject of 'Peace', but you can use any other subject that is appropriate to your evolving process.

Take a sheet of paper and put a circle in the middle with the word 'Peace' clearly written in it, thus:

Now quite simply think about this subject. Any words, images, ideas and so on that come to you as you think as one-pointedly as possible about this subject, put on lines radiating out from this circle. You might end up, for example, with something like the following diagram, but remember to find your own connections and not just copy these.

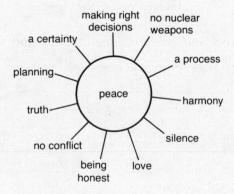

When you feel you have exhausted your thoughts on the subject of 'Peace', continue for at least another five minutes. This allows you to delve deeper than you normally might, accessing deeper recesses of your mind. Your knowledge of the subject, through this kind of reflection, is stretched.

RECEPTIVE MEDITATION

With receptive meditation, you tune into your unconscious and receive intuitions, inspirations, messages, energies, and stimuli about your chosen subject. The most important requisite for receptive meditation is silence, as without it you cannot hear what your inner world is telling you.

Perform your receptive meditation in as quiet an external place as possible, and make your inner world as silent as possible also. Hold the concept of 'Peace' in your consciousness and try not to think of anything else. Be one-pointed in your determination to shut off all extraneous thoughts, feelings and sensations. Just be.

Do not do anything, just see what comes to you. Meditate in this receptive way for at least fifteen minutes.

Before continuing, record anything that came to you during this meditation.

CREATIVE MEDITATION

Now consider what you have learned about 'Peace' from both your reflective and receptive meditations and in particular how you could put this knowledge and understanding into action. Try to find which of these ideas are the most relevant to you in your life right now, then choose one item from your meditation that you would like to put into action.

Consider this one concept. Find ways of acting upon it. Be precise and practical in this. For example, if you choose 'to be more loving' as your action to bring more Peace into manifestation, find ways to do this actively and practically. You might want to express your love to someone very directly, or alternatively you might simply want to do something for someone you know which will please them. Even the simplest acts, rightly performed with intention, can be very effective.

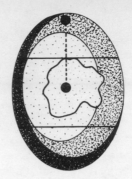

6 · PURPOSE AND THE CREATIVE WILL

*Since the outcome of successful willing is the satisfaction of
one's needs, we can see that the act of will is essentially
joyous. And the realisation of ... being a self ... gives a
sense of freedom, of power, of mastery which is profoundly
joyous.*

Roberto Assagioli

Every choice or decision we make is an act of will. We might
not be aware that we have chosen, and may even feel like a
total victim with no choice at all. Without making a choice, we
could not stay where we are or move anywhere else. Without
making a choice, we could not either stop what we are doing
or continue doing it. Our will power is the dynamic energy
that brings us into this world and if we consciously connect
with this energy it gives us the ability to be and do and become
whatever we wish.

We have many different inner powers and the right use of
these powers can enable us to make the best choices both for
our own well-being and the world around us. We can only
make these choices, however, through developing these inner
powers in a balanced and conscious way. The discovery of our
will and its subsequent training is the foundation of this work,

which can be best achieved through direct experience. If we make a comparison with a car, the first thing we have to learn is that there is an engine through which we can choose to move the car. Then we have to find ways of using that engine so that we can travel in the direction that is best for us at any given moment.

Of course, a lot of the time our actual experience is very different from this. Even if we are aware we have a car, it certainly doesn't feel like we are in the driving seat! We are drifting or muddling along as if we are the victims of our circumstances. We see ourselves as the victims of where we are or who we are, of poverty or depression, of failure or even success! We are the victims of other people who made us whatever we are, or stop us doing what we wish. Since childhood we have been told by parents and teachers and other 'well wishers' that we need to face the 'reality' of life. The message, that we cannot have everything we want, easily becomes one that says we cannot have anything we want.

If someone asks us to do something, the two obvious responses are yes and no. Yet usually we have a third choice available to us – 'not for now'. We do not have to limit ourselves by saying yes or no when 'not for now' is more appropriate. Sometimes it is right to make quick and immediate responses. The question at hand needs a fast response, or it is obvious which choice is needed. Often, however, we can take the time to consider our choices and make them in a more centred, balanced way. The more consciousness we bring into our decisions, the more we are able to choose what are the right decisions for us.

In psychosynthesis, we consider that any act of will actually takes place through six clear steps:

- investigation (finding out what it is we wish to do);
- deliberation (considering all the different things we wish to do at any time and selecting the acts most relevant to our current situation);
- decision (deciding upon the one act that is most important to us at the present time, and clearly formulating and stating this desire);

- affirmation (staying connected to this decision through constantly re-affirming that this choice is what we really desire to achieve);
- plan (thinking about the different ways we can actually make whatever it is happen);
- execution (doing it, finding ways of carrying out the intended plan, either in entirety or step by step.)

Every choice we make involves these six steps to a greater or lesser degree. It might be that for a particular choice we know what we want, hardly have to deliberate over it at all, and are able to plan quickly and execute the action necessary to succeed. For example, our choice to go to a nearby shop to purchase something we need. On the other hand, we might not really know what we want, and we might endlessly deliberate over the choices and never actually decide what to do. Or we might know exactly what we want and yet not know how to go about planning and executing the necessary actions. Our desire could be something well worked out, but for which the execution needs to take place at a particular time. If we choose a full moon, we will only be able to make it happen on the right night and at the right time.

Whilst our acts of will always include all the six steps, they rarely do so in a linear fashion. For instance, whilst planning we may need to go back and deliberate further when we discover that we have not quite got the choice right. Often we need to keep going back to our choice to affirm it over and over. Constantly returning to the affirmation stage to focus on and strengthen our choices is usually a good technique as it reinforces the planning and execution of our desire.

We also have to consider that every choice we make affects everything and everyone else. If I choose to eat this particular orange right now, you will never be able to eat it either now or at any other time. That may not seem so serious – after all, there are plenty more oranges. In other circumstances, however, such knowledge takes on much more significance. For example, someone may choose to ignore their knowledge that lead-free petrol is better for the environment. That they continue buying leaded petrol seems to make no difference, because after all what difference can one person make? Yet in reality the situation will surely be worsening.

We must make our choices clearly and with heart, and be aware of this global effect, yet we must not allow such knowledge to make us impotent. Rather we must try to align ourselves with the flow of nature so that our choices add to rather than subtract from the evolution of consciousness on our planet.

THE STAGES OF WILLING

Although the process is actually continuous, we can experience the will as having four stages. The first stage could be described as 'having no will'. It is a common human experience to feel like a victim to outside forces, other people or the circumstances in which we find ourselves. At many times in our lives we all experience a sense of impotency, frustration and an inability to act. Instead of doing what we wish, we become totally reactive to the circumstances or the environment. We feel as if what we are and what we are able to do or not do is totally dependent upon what happens outside of us.

At these times we act like a victim to our repressed urges and desires, to basic drives, or to people or events outside of us. When we are coming from this state, when we believe ourselves to be 'will-less', our primary motivations are desire and fear. We do not see ourselves as having any control, but instead experience ourselves as 'slaves of desire', whether we are fully conscious of this or not. Our one wish is to get our desires met and to avoid as much struggle, effort and pain as possible. If we have to manipulate people, we will, so long as our desires are met. As we reduce our responsibility in this way we become even more of a victim and we can easily sink further into this deadening trap.

In reality, however horrible the situation you are in may truly be, you can make of it what you will. You could be unjustly imprisoned and, as a victim, spend your days bemoaning your fate. You might plot revenge on those who unjustly imprisoned you, those to whom you are a victim. Or you could undertake some other plan of action – you could meditate, write, use the time to make detailed observations of yourself or your fellow inmates, and so on. There are many stories of people doing just this.

Of course, we do not have to be in such an extreme situation to feel like a victim. Think of times right now when you feel like a victim. Perhaps you are a victim to your boss at work, or to your partner, your parents, or even your children! Perhaps you feel like you are a victim to the unjust society in which you live. The key to releasing yourself from this victim consciousness is to realise that, whatever is happening to you, you are creating the situation. We all re-create our worlds afresh each and every moment.

The next stage of the will is understanding that 'will exists'. We might still feel we cannot actually do it, but we know, whatever it is, that it is possible. We realise we have a choice. Of course, we may have reached this stage with a part of our personality, and be more or less developed in other parts. Even if this stage of the will is only partially experienced, however, it leads to a shift in awareness from unconscious desires to active, conscious wishes. We might still feel separate, but there is a beginning of responsibility, of personal power, of the knowledge that choice is possible.

Once we know that the will exists we are able to start working on developing it within ourselves. There are two basic aspects of will power that we can develop and, in psychosynthesis, we call these 'the strong will' and 'the skilful will'. Strong will is the energy to choose whilst skilful will is the knowledge of how to use that energy. The strong will is like a car, the skilful will the driver. In most of us, one will be developed more than the other, but there is usually room for improvement in both.

One of the best ways to develop the strong will is to exercise it in your daily life. You may hate housework so to develop your will you could choose to do it regularly and with positive attention. You can choose to make physical acts into acts of will. If you were gardening, for instance, you could do it consciously, being aware that each spadeful of earth you move, or each flower you plant is an act of will.

You might do aerobic exercises, or dancing, and do this not so much just for the exercise value, but because you are consciously choosing to make each movement. You could choose to read stories or watch television programmes about great heroic deeds performed against all odds. You can easily devise other techniques for strengthening the strong will, but above all perform these techniques playfully, cheerfully and with interest.

You can also develop skilful will through acts in your daily life. When washing up, for example, you might ask yourself what is the most skilful way to do this, to make it most efficient and with the least expenditure of unnecessary energy? Should you wash the greasy pans or the glasses first? The development of skill is accomplished not only through what you actually do but through the attitude you have to the act being performed. It's not what you do, it's how you do it. Part of this skill is being aware of how much energy you put into doing something. If you put in too little energy, it's like using a spoon to move a mountain: using too much energy, like taking a forklift truck to an egg!

Once we have developed our will, at least to some degree, we pass to the next stage which is called 'having a will'. When this stage or level is attained, it can be experienced consciously or unconsciously, but it happens, usually, through a gradual awakening. We start to become a 'director' in our life. When we have chosen to play a particular role, we hold both an awareness of the self or centre, and the role which we are playing. We switch between them as appropriate.

When we consciously realise we have a will, there is a distinct move towards integration. There is less fragmentation and more clarity of choice. We start to feel more connected to our 'purpose' for being alive on this planet at this time, and we truly take responsibility for our acts. Of course, we may not be responsible and conscious in this way all of the time, but the amount of time we spend in this state gradually starts to increase.

In psychosynthesis we call the fourth and final stage of the evolution of the will in the individual 'being will'. When this stage is reached there is alignment with the transpersonal

Self and the deepest, most spiritual aspects of will. We are connected with our innermost understanding. We can reach this level of consciousness through meditation, through silence, or simply through turning inwards and allowing this energy of the Self to permeate through us. Once we have reached this stage, even for a moment, it is inevitable that we will desire to express this deep and meaningful connection in the outside world. Indeed, it is the sign of true 'spiritual attainment' not when the person involved can sit for hours in a yoga posture, or perform 'miraculous' feats, but rather when this energy is expressed in the world in a way that brings healing and sustenance to his or her fellow beings.

SPIRITUAL PURPOSE

When we start using our will from a centred place, we become the cause of what happens in our life and are not just an effect of or victim to circumstances. We discover there is a distinction between our 'true will' or Purpose, which can be defined as the will of the Self, and the energies, such as drives and self-centred desires, that come from subpersonalities. This is not to say that subpersonalities should not get what they want; their needs have to be met fully before they can truly be transformed. But their wishes are inevitably in conflict with the wishes of other subpersonalities. We experience no such conflicts with the 'true will' for this originates from the deepest, innermost core of our being.

We can only truly discover our true will or Purpose when we consciously and actively take steps towards its manifestation. That may seem obvious, but too often we forget this and, instead of following our path a step at a time, we try to leap ahead, not paying attention to what is happening in the present moment. The next step is always of utmost importance and, in actuality, the only step we can make. Even physically if we try to take four steps at once we are more likely to fall over than succeed. This is even more true when we are talking about inner Purpose. We find it is easier to stay on our path if we pay attention to our immediate position, rather than worrying about something a long way ahead.

We may have little or no idea of what our true will or Purpose is, but if we reflect upon what Purpose means to us, and what we would like to manifest in our lives that has 'real meaning', we can start getting at least an inkling of it. You might like to try some reflective, receptive and creative meditation on 'Purpose'. Remember that Purpose always follows the rule of non-interference – it cannot be your real Purpose if it involves you interfering with or altering someone else's Purpose.

When we have connected to our Purpose – through meditation as suggested above, or through any of the other methods used in psychosynthesis or other ways to self realisation – the next step is to decide how to manifest this Purpose. The techniques for grounding which we have already discussed can be most helpful in this, but the most important thing is to find our own individual ways of manifesting our Purpose. This is where it is often most helpful to have a good guide who will not only be able to help us connect with our Purpose but will also help us find ways to manifest it.

THE GOOD WILL

The will is not only active, not only involved with 'doing'. You could choose, for example, to just be, to pass some time 'doing nothing'. Indeed, one of the greatest distortions in our thinking about will power is to believe it has to be an effort or strenuous, or that it uses up energy in some way. On the contrary, when we make conscious, definite acts of will, rather than ending up with less energy, we feel energised, more alive, more 'present' in the world.

Sometimes it is right to act and sometimes it is right to just let things be. To do the latter is no less an act of will, and in fact can sometimes require much more effort. For example, people who are naturally very wilful often find it difficult to be receptive and simply surrender to what is happening without the need to control or interfere.

We need to be flexible and able to find a balance between active and passive acts of will. Both can require strong and skilful will. To say 'no' to something, for instance, might require a tremendous act of courage if friends are encouraging you to do it. Or to exhibit patience in waiting for something you madly desire can require great reserves of strong will. The more centred we become, the more able we are to make acts of will, either active or passive, strong or skilful, as the situation requires.

One result of moving towards our centre and making our acts of will more conscious and purposeful is that we find there is another aspect of the will, sometimes called 'the good will'. Acts of will that are made from the heart, that are filled with sympathy, love, understanding and warmth, are all manifestations of the good will. When we have good will towards someone, whether we act upon it or not, we are connecting the energy of the will with the energy of love.

Psychosynthesis sees the good will as a synthesis of the archetypes or energies of love and will. An act of good will made towards someone is a dynamic and joy-filled process that fosters understanding and co-operation. When we tune into the good will we recognise that whatever we do, it is part of the greater whole of human relations. The good will has also been described as 'love in action'. In terms of human relations, so long as we only do to others what we would have them do to us, we are tuning into the energy of the good will. The good will, however, is not just being soft and nice, it is dynamic and active.

Imagine what we would like if we had no good will at all. We would not be able to express love actively, we would take actions that promoted our own interests at the expense of others, we might be suspicious and defensive, judgmental, prejudiced, indifferent to the suffering of others, isolated and so on. On the other hand, we could have too much good will. People would walk all over us, or we might be overly helpful to the point of interference, or we might never be able to say no. We would be so nice we would be really sugary sweet.

With just the right amount of good will, however, we create a true balance between both love and will, we are co-operative and helpful and exhibit all the qualities of 'right human relations'. At each and every moment, all of us have the choice as to whether we want to exhibit good will or not. As always we have three options – yes, no, or not for now. Right now we can choose which of these options we wish to take. If we choose to say 'yes' to the good will, there will naturally be times when we do not succeed. But whenever this happens, we can always choose to come back to it, centring ourselves again and becoming once more enthused with its energy.

EXERCISE: THE VALUE OF THE WILL

Relax and centre yourself. Think of times in your life when you have missed an opportunity or caused pain to yourself or someone else through your lack of will or purpose, or your inability to either make clear choices or act upon them. Picture these events as vividly as possible and allow the associated feelings to affect you.

Now write down a list of these times in your life with which you have just connected. Let yourself really desire to change yourself so that you have more will.

Reflect on all the opportunities and benefits there would be both for yourself and others if your will was strengthened. Think clearly what these advantages would be, then write them down. Allow the feelings aroused by these anticipated advantages to really affect you. Feel the joy that these opportunities could give you, the satisfaction you would feel if you were more strong willed. Let yourself really feel your desire to become stronger in this way.

Finally picture yourself as having a strong will. Imagine yourself acting in every situation with firm decisions, focused intention, and clear awareness. Visualise yourself walking, talking, sitting and simply being in a way that exhibits your connection with your will. You are strong, yet subtle, firm yet kind, acting with skill and discrimination. Realise you can use this technique to strengthen your will whenever you choose.

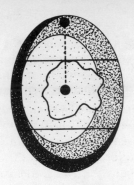

7 · THE POWER OF IMAGINATION

Imagine the conditions of the world when the majority is concerned with the good of others and not with its own selfish goals. Realise the part that you can play in building this world. Visualise the spirit of goodwill as a ray of light reaching out from you ... to all people, problems, and situations that are your immediate concern.

Roberto Assagioli

Imagination is our ability to form images or concepts of external objects that are not actually present to our senses, or are even non-existent. We can imagine a unicorn, for example, yet it is unlikely many of us have actually seen one! Imagination is thus the basis of the creative faculties of the mind. Anything that is created, whether artistically, scientifically or in any other way, is initially conceived of in imagination. In psychosynthesis, we use imagination to explore our unconscious inner processes and to stimulate our personal, interpersonal and transpersonal growth. We also use imagination to express this inner learning and growth in our outer world in creative and life-enhancing ways.

Imagination offers us a symbolic connection to our

unconscious, and can help us connect with all our unconscious processes. Once we make this connection, transformation is possible. Imagination can also help us to understand and express our inner wisdom in a stimulating way. Through using imagination to connect to our inner processes, we can bring underdeveloped parts of ourselves out into the open where they can gain independence. In fact, our imaginative faculties not only offer us a symbolic connection with our inner world, they can help us transform all our inner and outer relationships.

Although some images may be seen as universal, each one of us has our own world of imagery. To many of us today a white dove may symbolise 'peace', yet it may not only symbolise 'food' but actually be an item of food to someone else. In the West we may wear black to a funeral, yet in other parts of the world white is worn. This is not to deny the importance of universal symbolism, through which we can make rich and rewarding connections. But it is of utmost importance we find our own images and symbols and trust in our own inner processes. What something means to you has much more significance than any interpretation put on it by someone else. In psychosynthesis we always encourage people to find their own imagery and find their own personal connection to symbols and myths.

When we start exploring the images that come up from our unconscious, it inevitably expands our awareness. There has to be a balance between this awareness and the will, however. The new images that emerge may expand our awareness about ourselves and our world, but we need the will to do something about this awareness. If we do not integrate our increasing awareness we run the risk of becoming 'image junkies', always on the look out for new images and symbols as if they were a drug feeding a false sense of 'self'. This can then inflate us and separate us from any true connections to the transpersonal. On the other hand, if we do not explore the realms of imagery and symbols, but try to rely on what we already know, see and feel, then we run the equally dangerous risk of becoming rigid and sterile.

There are many ways of using the imagination. For example, in imagination we can try things out in a symbolic way. Both real and imaginary situations that frighten us can be accessed and worked on before the actual situation (for example, an interview) happens. We can use our imagination to change our relationship with different aspects of ourselves. Indeed, the many different ways of using our imagination to help us grow are only limited by the powers of our imagination. Anything we can imagine could possibly happen – and we can imagine just about anything.

Another use of imagery is to relive past experiences (whether 'highs' or 'lows'). If we allow ourselves to relive a traumatic experience and fully allow the feelings, emotions and sensations that accompany the images associated with the experience, there is a possibility of transformation. When an old pattern is removed we can 'make space' for a new pattern. If you relive, through imagery, your birth, for instance, and clear out some of the pain and difficulties associated with this experience, you could then use images and symbols to re-create a 'new birth' that is healthier and more life-enhancing. Such use of imagery, so long as it is truly accompanied by the associated experiences, can have a profound transformative effect on our personalities.

The power of the imagination is well-known to advertisers, big business, politicians, and all those who would control or manipulate us in some way. If we see the same advertisement many times over and get bored with it and think the advertiser would do better to change it, then we are missing the point. Even if we consciously resist it, anything that is repeatedly presented to our senses has an effect. We may not think we bought a certain product as a result of advertising, yet in many cases we have done just that, albeit totally unconsciously. All images and symbols that we see or imagine tend to produce the physical conditions and external acts that correspond to them.

The fact that images repeated over and over sink into our unconscious, as it were, and affect us, can be used to our advantage. If we are affected by adverts in this way then we can choose to create our own adverts and respond to them.

For instance, if you wanted to have more love in your life you might write a suitable affirmation on some cards – 'I am worthy of love' perhaps – and stick them up around your house in places where you will frequently see them. You won't have to consciously look at these messages for, just like other 'adverts', they will work on an unconscious level. Then, if you become more worthy of love, it is quite likely you will get more of it!

Through images, it is also possible to manifest positive qualities in your everyday life. If we used this power to contact, say, the quality of Joy and manifest more of it onto our planet it would be most positive. Symbols can help us discover and utilise our power. To connect with our power in this way we need to use our discriminative faculties to ensure we only manifest what is 'for the highest good'. When we truly own our power, and align ourselves through our sense of self with our Purpose, as described in the last chapter, we find we naturally discriminate with an easy inner wisdom.

We can use our imagination to manifest our power in many different ways. We can start, for example, with a given image, such as the meadow or the mountain found in many of the exercises used in psychosynthesis. Sometimes we might just like to relax and let the images flow, trusting in the wisdom of our unconscious to bring up what is right for us at any given moment in time. Any way we choose to use images to aid our growth is effective if it comes naturally and is not forced. As our imagination is so rich we need never force anything, but we do have to learn to trust in ourselves.

We can find real joy in moulding the contents of our unconscious, controlling our inner world in a positive way, not so that we have 'power over' anything or anyone, but so that we have 'power with' the true nature of our inner being. When we start finding our inner freedom, when we are no longer controlled by images and fantasies but are able to use them for our own advantage, in an unselfish way, we are becoming psychologically mature.

All kinds of images, positive and negative, are continuously emerging from our unconscious. We can react to them or we can act upon them. In other words, we can have them or let them have us. If we have them then we can do what we want with them. We can feed upon the positive images, letting them grow bigger and stronger, and we can disperse the negative ones, not letting them take us over. For instance, we can quite simply take a positive image that is emerging from our unconscious, and consciously choose to make it grow bigger and bigger, letting it overwhelm us and fill us with its positive energy. On the other hand, when a negative image emerges from our unconscious, we can cause it to grow smaller and smaller until it disappears. We could even imagine it is totally consumed in the light of a burning, cleansing sun.

If we let ourselves go, and trust in the emerging images from our unconscious, we can have a sense of being 'new born'. We become more able to connect with the 'newness' of any situation without becoming identified or attached to what is happening.

THE ESSENCE OF SYMBOLS

Symbols are the 'language of the unconscious'. When we start communicating with our inner world, we do so through symbols. To be truly understood and integrated, however, symbols cannot just be understood on an intellectual level but must also arouse feelings and sensations. Neither can they be understood or interpreted out of context. A plane dropping bombs and a plane delivering needed supplies not only involve different concepts of 'plane' (although the same plane can do both jobs), but also arouse totally different feelings. To truly understand a symbol we have to get behind the outer form, which can veil and hide the inner meaning, and tune into the inner truth, the essence of the symbol.

In psychosynthesis, we are not so concerned with cold, rational analysis of symbols but rather choose to approach this essential inner form. Some of the basic ways of achieving this include:

- simply considering the outermost form of the symbol, seeing what it shows you on its surface without any analysis or interpretation at all. It is often surprising and illuminating to discover that the symbols that emerge spontaneously from our unconscious often tell us so much just in themselves, without us needing to interpret or judge them in any way.

- allowing the feelings and emotions that the symbol brings up to be fully experienced. Again we can do this most effectively when we suspend judgement and interpretation. Feelings are truly about values, so when we allow ourselves to 'feel' a symbol we discover its true value.

- using our intellectual skills to discover what a symbol teaches us, penetrating into the deepest meaning of the symbol. Without having to analyse a symbol rationally we can use our thinking function to bring our knowledge into play and interpret the symbol in a clear and non-judgmental way.

- letting the symbol's inner or deeper meaning intuitively emerge. Behind any of the sensations, feelings and thoughts we may have about any symbol is its more abstract, 'bigger' meaning, an understanding that goes beyond our individual concepts about it. We cannot learn to be intuitive, we can only 'let it happen'. When it does we are then tuning into levels where we are more deeply in tune with the Purpose of our soul.

- identifying with the symbol. To discover the quality and purpose of a symbol we can choose to identify with it. The form in which a symbol manifests may obscure its deepest meaning or it may not, but in either case, through identifying ourselves with the symbol we can start to connect with its deepest essence. To do this effectively we have to be centred and relaxed, and not attached to any of the thoughts, feelings or even intuitions we may already have about it. For example, you could do the Self Identification exercise and then consciously imagine you are the symbol under investigation. What then do you think, feel and sense?

We can change both our inner fantasy world and the outer 'reality' on an individual and collective level. The symbols with which we need to work never have to be suggested from outside, as our unconscious will invariably send us the right messages. When we can trust these messages from our inner world, we find they are transformative both to us as individuals and, through us, to our world as a whole. We can re-own symbols so they are part of the life-enhancing process of growth and evolution rather than leave them in the hands of those who would use them to control and manipulate others for their own selfish ends.

DREAMING

Because dreaming does not 'actually happen' in the outer world but, by its very nature, only happens in imagination, we can see that it plays an important part in how our unconscious speaks to us. As with all the work we do with symbols in psychosynthesis, although there are times when we need to analyse the symbolic content of our dreams, we often find we learn best what they are trying to tell us about ourselves if we use other, less directly analytical methods.

We can take any item from a dream, whether a person or an inanimate object or whatever, and have a conversation with this item, letting it speak and give us useful information. Try remembering a recent dream right now and, taking any item from the dream, speak to it and then see what it has to say back to you. Another way of working with dreams is to consciously continue with the dream's contents. This is particularly useful if a dream feels incomplete in any way. We can allow ourselves to imagine what happens next, letting the 'story' of the dream unfold until it comes to a positive, life-enhancing conclusion.

It is sometimes useful to draw or paint images from dreams. Doing this, we often receive deep insights into the meaning of our dreams without imposing any kind of intellectual interpretation. For instance, we might start to recognise recurring themes in our dreams, which may help us to see things that we are attached to or with which we need to work further in some way.

When we 'awake', as it were, within a dream and become aware that we are dreaming whilst still in the dream, it is called lucid dreaming. Within lucid dreams, unlike their more usual counterparts, we can make deliberate acts.

Perhaps the simplest method to induce lucid dreaming is if we tell ourselves, as we drop off to sleep, that we are able to have lucid dreams! This affirmation is then planted in our unconscious and helps create the conditions for lucid dreams. We cannot expect it to happen every time, however, and we may need to continuously repeat the formula for many weeks or months before success is achieved.

Whether we have any lucid dreams or not, it is always useful to watch dreams, looking particularly for patterns in the events of dreams that help us understand our relationship to our unconscious. Keeping a dream journal in which we record our dreams upon awakening also increases our perception. When we realise that we spend a third of our life in sleep, it becomes almost second nature to accept that the events we remember from dreams are worthy of our attention. Dreams are messages from our unconscious realms. Most dreams, it is generally believed, are simply re-plays of 'stuff' from our lower unconscious, based on past incidents and events which our consciousness is trying to understand or restructure in some way. Working on these dreams, therefore, can be a potent way to work with our lower unconscious. Occasionally we have dreams whose origin appears to be the superconscious. These dreams often have a particularly luminous quality to them, and we feel subjectively different about their quality. When we get such dreams, which can include prophetic visions and deep spiritual insights, it is not so much a matter of working with them, but rather of holding the vision and allowing ourselves to see it unfold in a natural, organic way.

EXERCISE: THE HOUSE OF THE SELF

When we use any kind of imagery, we are making a connection between the conscious and the unconscious. To make such a connection real in our everyday lives it is important to connect all these images with our body. We can also use our bodies as a source of symbols and images. How does your body feel at this moment? We can use these images creatively in our personal growth. In the following exercise, we will use our imagination to see our inner world in a concrete form. So long as we keep it on this level, however, it will not be as real as if we find ways to ground our insights and understanding through our bodies and out into the world.

Make yourself comfortable, relax and centre yourself. Imagine you are a house. See yourself as a house. What kind of house are you – a cottage, a terraced house, a grand mansion or what? Take some time to imagine what sort of house you are in as much detail as possible.

Picture this house in front of you and imagine you enter through the front door. This is no problem, for it is your house. You can explore the rest of the house some other time, but for now we will visit the basement or cellar.

Find the way down to the basement, and consider what it is like. Go into as much detail as you can, from assessing the condition of the foundations, the walls of the basement, the damp level, what junk might be stored there, and so on. Assess whatever comes up so you get a good, clear picture of the full state of your basement. Really be as honest as if you were a surveyor checking the house for possible purchase.

Now recall it is your house and choose to do with it whatever you like. Change the basement in any way that seems suitable to you. Perhaps you need to reinforce the walls, or dry it out, or paint it, or throw away junk – take some time to make your basement into the sort of basement you would most like to have. The power of your imagination will even allow you to add or remove rooms, completely change the shape or style of the basement, make of it what you will.

When you are ready and have made whatever changes you desire to your house, bring yourself back to everyday consciousness and write about your experience in your workbook or diary.

If you think about the psychosynthesis egg diagram and relate this to the house you have just imagined, it is quite easy to see how by exploring the basement in this way you have been exploring some aspects of your lower unconscious. At other times you can explore other parts of the 'house', including 'going upstairs' to explore your superconscious. Remember, however, that whatever you may find upstairs or downstairs, it becomes really useful when you bring it into your everyday life, the 'living room' of your house, and use it in a way that assists your growth and development. What did you discover in your basement that it would be useful for you to bring up to the living room and utilise in some way?

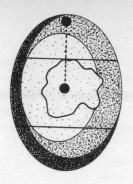

8 · Acceptance and Change

In accepting pleasure without craving for it and attachment to it, and in accepting pain, when unavoidable, without fearing it and rebelling against it, one can learn much from both pleasure and pain, and 'distil the essence' which they contain.

Roberto Assagioli

If we become attached to change and try to make things in our lives change before they are ready, we are fighting a losing battle. Similarly, if we become attached to things staying the same and resist all changes in our lives, the battle is similarly hard and ultimately pointless. On the other hand, if we learn to accept what is happening without being identified either with things changing or staying the same, this creates the space in our lives for things to either change or not as appropriate.

Two primary, archetypal energies in life are 'change' and 'maintenance'. Both are equally necessary, and both form part of a dynamic polarity of energy with which we can either co-operate or not. When we accept either, then these energies can manifest through us in a relatively undistorted way. Change can then be seen in terms of progress, evolution, transformation, and freedom. Maintenance, in this clear form, manifests as timelessness, rhythm, patience and a sense of eternity.

When we fight either change or maintenance and do not accept things as they are, then these energies start manifesting in a more distorted way. Then change can be purposeless, lead to the dissipation of our energy, make us insensible to either our needs or the needs of others, be destructive and leave us without proper and clear boundaries. Maintenance, once distorted, leads to inertia and laziness, closed-mindedness, rigidity, cowardice and fear of the unknown, and a strangulation of the flow of life energy.

It cannot be over-emphasized that there is a need for both change and maintenance in our lives. When we talk about acceptance of what is, and allowing both of these polarities to manifest in our lives, this does not mean we have to accept blindly some predestined fate, or make ourselves victims to circumstances. On the contrary, when we learn the value of true inner acceptance, this frees our energy so that we can either change or not as is best for us in any particular set of circumstances. Of course it is not always so easy, but it is for us to balance ourselves in a way that excludes neither change or maintenance, but includes the best of both.

Everything changes all the time. This is a basic truth of life. If we could accept this 'truth', then we would not become so fearful when events in our lives do not appear to be changing fast enough – or appear to be changing too fast. We would be able to see that, as everything changes, these things too – whatever 'these things' are – will pass away. We might feel trapped in a relationship that no longer serves us – but everything changes. We might feel alone because we cannot find a good relationship – but everything changes. We would be able to tune into the natural flow of life and accept what is. Then we would be able to act from this place and let things come or go as appropriate.

This is all very well but, in reality, for most of us we often become attached to or identified with our desire for certain things to change and certain things to stay the same. You have a good relationship – well, of course you don't want it to change, but if you hold onto it and don't let it grow and change in its natural fashion then it will become rigidified. Then it will not be the same relationship anyway, and the chances are it will change, perhaps now in a way you wouldn't want. Or maybe you are not in a relationship and you want things to change so badly you become attached beyond anything else to the idea of having a partner. You yearn for it and, at every opportunity, you make allegiances and try hard to make it work. Often people doing this find that they are trying so hard it just doesn't happen, or if it does, it doesn't last. Once more the attachment has led you astray, and life isn't 'working' again!

Once we let go of our attachment to anything changing or to anything staying the same, however, we start to see it for what it really is. With this new vision of how something is, we can choose to change it or not from a clearer perspective. But this true acceptance has to be really felt, really lived, it cannot just be an intellectual position. Then, once acceptance is experienced in this way, transformation can take place.

When we accept life in this dynamic way, not simply resigning ourselves to circumstances but actively and consciously realising we are choosing them, we are more able to understand their inner meaning for us. When we accept something in this way we more clearly see it for what it is. We then have the choice of either letting it happen or fighting it in a more effective way.

We can never totally get rid of unwanted experiences in our life so we may as well learn to accept them. Indeed, it is many people's experience that if they fight against unwanted experiences the situation just becomes worse. On the other hand, if we accept that life does include pain and failure, unpleasant experiences and times when we have to do things we would rather not do, we take control of the energy and can use it for rather than against us. For example, if we accept that we are feeling depressed, we become more able to deal with it effectively than if we do not accept it and try to shrug it off.

We cannot always change the outer conditions but we can always work on the inner conditions. It may seem paradoxical if we simply think about it, but once we act upon it we find that the one way we always have available to us of causing change is through an act of acceptance. When we accept what is, we are open to learn. Understood in this way, acceptance is one of the most major tools for transformation.

If we think of a recent experience that we really enjoyed and recall all the features of this experience, the pleasure associated with this good experience, whatever it was, will come up into our consciousness. It is possible to relive pleasurable experiences, to feel them inside as if they are still happening. This is a healthy act, something that can give us pleasure and make us feel good. Problems arise, however, once we become so attached to it that it is all we want and we devote all our energies to making it happen again.

On the other hand, if we recall a recent 'bad' experience, something we did not feel good about at the time, and spend some time recalling all the sensing, feeling and thinking associated with this experience, we can also feel this experience as if it is still happening. This, too, is a healthy act because, although we might not want to remember unpleasant or upsetting times in our lives, if we allow ourselves the space to do so, it can help us deal with the associated issues.

Both apparently positive and apparently negative experiences in our lives can be viewed as having value. Indeed, it is often the learning we get from the supposedly 'unwanted' experiences that helps us to grow the most and become able to express who we really are and what we actually want in life. To really delve into the depths of our past and bring to the surface traumatic or upsetting experiences is work best done in the presence of a good therapist or guide. But as we learn to accept the value of both types of experience, we become more complete in ourselves, and more able to face the future, whatever it brings us.

THE POWER TO ACCEPT AND CHANGE

We can use the powers of will and imagination to make things change, or to accept things as they are. To do either we have to have the will to make it happen, whether actively causing change or passively letting things unfold. We also need imagination so that we can create the new worlds into which we wish to move, or change the old patterns from our past. We have learnt about using both these powers in previous chapters of this book. They are sometimes described as the powers that give us the ability to cause change to occur in the way we want it to. They are also the powers that help us to accept times when it is right for things not to change.

To make this work effectively we also need the powers of love and awareness. Without awareness how could we know whether our choice is 'right' or not? And without love how could we be sure we were making the 'right' choice in accordance with the needs and energies of other people? These four energies – love, awareness, will and imagination – are those we use throughout our lives to aid us in taking the actions we want, and that are in accord with the evolution of consciousness on the planet.

These energies become particularly important to us when we are at a time of pain or crisis. Such experiences are often what lead us to find help from a psychosynthesis guide or from some other kind of therapist or counsellor. In psychosynthesis we do not attempt to 'patch up' the pain, divert the crisis or ignore the failure. On the contrary, we realise the value in such experiences. It is often through accepting pain, in all its guises, that we come to realise more about ourselves and unleash creative energies.

We all have the experience of failure at some time or another in our lives. Many people experience failure so often that they start to see themselves as 'a failure'. Then it is as if failure has got them rather than them having it! No longer does a person in this state say, 'I have a situation in my life where I have failed' but the experience takes hold and they say something more akin to, 'I am a failure.' When we experience failure it can cause us to cut off from our potential energy. For example, we may be angry, bitter or disappointed. It is fine to feel these things, but it is also important, when we are ready, to move on, to allow the creative potential to flow once more. We can take the initial stage towards achieving this through simply accepting the failure and the resultant emotional turmoil.

One of the most powerful techniques for doing this is called 'blessing the obstacle'. In order to accept the failure, we make a conscious act of blessing whatever has stopped us from succeeding. Once we have done this, not just through paying 'lip service' to the concept but through actually taking on this attitude as completely as possible, we are ready to move on.

When we consider what we have learned from the apparent 'failure', then the idea of 'blessing the obstacle' is not such a strange concept. It is similar to the concept of loving your enemy. For instance, a failure will have given us the opportunity to try again whatever it was we 'failed at', only better this time. If it were some act that could never happen again, then through blessing the obstacle we can come to the realisation that it obviously was not meant to happen. In doing this we are not subordinating ourselves to some impersonal fate, but rather we are making an act of conscious control and decision-making.

Everything we do in our lives, whether we are conscious of it this way or not, we decide. Even if that is not an actual 'truth' there is nothing to stop us believing it is true. If we choose everything in our lives, then if it doesn't happen, we must have decided upon that, too. This can be hard to grasp and accept in our everyday consciousness, as our personalities have not been conscious of the process and certain subpersonalities may even want to hold onto the pain or failure. But in psychosynthesis we always believe that at the level of the self or soul we decide upon everything that happens to us in life.

If we can learn to surrender to pain rather than sinking deeper into it and becoming overwhelmed with the experience, we will find that we move through it more quickly. But the first stage has to be to surrender to the experience, to let it happen completely. This is easier said than done, of course, but once we achieve this we can consciously choose to move on. Then, instead of being a victim to pain we always have the ability to ask ourselves: what use is this to me? What can I learn from it?

The crises we experience in life, although we may not see it so clearly when we are in a crisis, actually put us up against our growing edge. Crises usually happen when we have an old pattern of behaviour or belief that no longer truly serves us and it would be better for us to let go of it. More often than not it is fear that stops us naturally doing this. Then the energy builds up until, if we are still resisting the change, we enter a crisis. It is as if the crisis, or at least its energy, originates in the superconscious and then 'knocks at the door' of the personality. We can either open the door or resist, and the longer we resist, the stronger the energy becomes until finally, if it is necessary, the energy will burst the door open anyway and we will enter into a life crisis.

Any new energy that is trying to emerge into our awareness has to be first accepted, then grounded and expressed. We often hold back from this out of fear. We may not exactly like things how they currently are but we'd rather face the devil we know than risk unleashing the unknown. We create blocks to the expression of our new, emerging energies, blocks that are often no more than simply fear of change. So the energy of crisis is really our survival energy which has been energised as a resistance to the new experience. It is only when we get far enough into it that we realise our survival truly requires us to change. Then we are able to accept the new situation and move on.

The most important aspect of this work is often not what is happening but our reaction to it – so turn and face it, whatever it is. At the same time dis-identify from the situation to gain a better perspective and a sense of right proportion. See both successes and failures for what they are – events in the unfolding of who you are. Gain a sense of perspective and proportion when you consider either, and always ask yourself: what choices can I make? How can I improve this in terms of my unfolding creative potential?

THE TRANSFORMATION OF ENERGY

If we do not accept pain, failure and crisis in our lives we often find energy building up in us that then may start to discharge itself in inappropriate ways. We may become overly aggressive, for example, and explode at little things, totally out of all proportion to what is actually happening. Or we may project our aggression, fear and pain onto other people, particularly members of our family, friends or work colleagues.

We all have the tendency in such situations to project onto other people our attitudes, impulses, and feelings. If we feel hostile towards someone, for instance, it is easy to project this hostility onto them and believe it is they who are being aggressive, not ourselves. We then in turn become defensive and threatened and a vicious circle is set up. If we perceive this happening we must take action to 're-own the projection'.

We have to accept the basic truth of life that everything depends upon our attitude. If we are feeling hostile to someone, or we perceive (correctly or incorrectly) that they are hostile to us, the only way we have to change this situation is through changing ourselves. We have to realise we have free will and can make the decision to be ourselves without making demands upon others or without projecting our 'stuff' onto them. We are then free to relate to them from a more centred position. When we do this we often find the situation transforms and the conflict is resolved.

It is often surprising to find how effective this can be. All we may need to do is simply share how we are feeling with the other people involved. If we are honest and let ourselves speak freely about our fears, our feelings, and our thoughts on whatever the conflict or issue is, we find the energy transforms. Suddenly we are friends again, sharing in the common plight of all humans, of being alone in essence and yet connected to everyone and everything at the same time. Such moments of true spiritual realisation, which can emerge out of the simplest act such as speaking up about our feelings, are truly transforming and enriching to our lives.

The important point in all this is that we are able to discharge the energies involved. It is the same if we feel true physical aggression. We do not have to go round to that person's house, for example, and get into a physical fight – we can quite simply beat hell out of a cushion. The satisfaction from doing this, coupled with the actual, physical discharge of energy, will clear our consciousness and we will be able to move forward with clearer choices and more awareness.

EXERCISE: BLESSING THE OBSTACLE

Choose to sit somewhere where you are relaxed but not so relaxed that you will fall asleep. Take a few deep breaths and centre yourself in whatever way you choose.

Remember a recent time where you experienced pain or failure in your life. Really consider this time in depth, allowing yourself to recall and experience all the associated thoughts, feelings and sensations. Let yourself really experience the pain associated with the experience.

Now imagine you step out of this experience so that you can see its elements laid out before you. Say out loud: 'I bless this (fear or whatever it was you experienced as pain or failure)'.

Continue to look at the components of this experience as if you are a detached observer of the pain, failure or whatever it is. Make the blessing statement out loud a couple of more times, and now as you do this see and feel the memory of the experience change. Let it become lighter and less attached to you.

Be aware of what you have learned from the situation, and then consciously choose to move on.

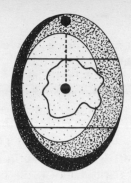

9 · BODY AND SELF

The body and psyche can be transmuted by means of a regenerative transformation. This produces an organic and harmonious unification . . . a bio-psychosynthesis.

Roberto Assagioli

One of the major and most valid criticisms of psychosynthesis in the past has been its exclusion of the physical body as anything more than a vehicle for imagery and grounding. There is no reason why psychosynthesis should exclude bodywork, however, and some modern psychosynthesis practitioners with a more holistic vision are now introducing many varied body techniques into their work. These include the more 'traditional' psychosynthetic use of the body as a source of images with which symbolic release may be achieved, and more direct, body-related techniques such as ones borrowed from bioenergetics, integrative body psychotherapy and other body-orientated methods of growth and development. It is also possible to use dance, massage, martial arts such as t'ai chi and other quite distinct methods of body awareness in a psychosynthesis context. As with all areas of psychosynthesis therapy, some of the most imaginative guides constantly devise ways of integrating body work, directly relating to the needs of their individual clients.

It has been argued that the Self Identification exercise which says 'I have a body, but I am not my body' involves a denial of the body. This is not the case, however – it is used in a context where the feelings and thoughts are treated in the same fashion, not to deny them but so that the individual can have a direct experience of dis-attached awareness. In fact, it is always stressed by good psychosynthesis guides how important it is to re-identify with the thoughts, feelings and body. Although people who tend to be a bit 'up in the clouds' and out of their bodies are often attracted to it, this position is most definitely not encouraged in psychosynthesis. The Self Identification exercise clearly includes the body when it says: 'My body is my precious instrument of experience and action in the outer world . . . I treat it well, I seek to keep it in good health, but it is not myself.' Indeed, we cannot truly dis-identify from something unless we *have* it first. In other words, it is actually the case that unless we have our bodies (as well as our feelings and thoughts), we cannot truly dis-identify from them, and therefore cannot truly achieve a personal psychosynthesis.

We often neglect and deny our bodies their proper place as 'the temple of our incarnation'. It is only through having a body that we can be here in the world, being and doing whatever it is we choose to be and do. But this neglect is a symptom of modern life generally, and not just psychosynthesis. The general trend in our Western societies is to eat convenience foods and unbalanced diets rather than listen to our real body needs. We are often more concerned about outer appearance and current fashions than the real health of our bodies. Exercise, if taken, is a fashionable fad rather than an essential part of healthy living.

We not only neglect the body, we often have distorted awareness about it. We become conditioned in childhood to associate shame and guilt with our bodies and some of our bodily functions. How often are children labelled 'dirty' for simply discovering an interest in their natural bodily instincts and functions? How often are children given conscious or unconscious messages of denial when they discover their natural sexuality? How often are we all denied access to the pleasures of the world of sensation? Yet it is patently true that if we reject our bodies or have distorted beliefs about our bodily sensations and functions, we will not be able to either fully dis-identify from or identify with our bodies.

When we are children we depend upon our parents for our basic physical survival. Ideally, we know our parents tried to do their best to love and protect us, but this does not deny the truth that they also hurt us physically and emotionally. We found ways to protect ourselves from this hurt. One of the chief ways we discovered for doing this was through building for ourselves a physical 'body armour'. This could protect us both from physical hurt and emotional and mental pain, inflicted not only by our parents but by other people as well. We needed this armour to protect us, but unfortunately we still wear it as adults. We are so encased and entrapped within it that we can only lift it off a bit at a time and then with great effort.

Psychosynthesis can teach us that we do not have to be attached to these defence mechanisms, this armour, for we are no longer children. As conscious adults we can choose to sense, feel and think without fear of denial or disapproval. Or if we get these reactions from other people we can accept their position without letting it overcome us and make us feel vulnerable. If we want to have a certain feeling, whether it makes us happy or sad, then we can have it without fear or guilt. So long as we do not harm anyone else with our actions, then we are truly free from these restrictions.

We can perform everyday physical acts, such as cleaning the house or doing the cooking, with a new awareness if we are more able to be in our bodies. Psychosynthesis won't help us actually cook a meal. But holding the vision of psychosynthesis and making our physical actions, whatever they are, from the consciousness of this vision, can help us cook, clean, make love, dance, be strong or be weak, as is right for any given situation. We can use psychosynthesis techniques not to sidestep physical reality or dis-attach from it, but to be really present in it by choosing to identify with it clearly and consciously. This is perhaps the clearest spiritual statement anyone can make. The spirit in psychosynthesis is seen as both transcendent and immanent. To be transcendent is to 'rise above' or go beyond ordinary, everyday reality, and to look 'for the spirit' or illumination in things not of this world. To be immanent is to invoke or 'draw down' the spirit into everyday reality, to find illumination in the mundane. On the transcendent side we may like to sit and meditate, but to 'do psychosynthesis' in everyday life we have to bring a sense of the immanent self into our lives. Then everything we do can be illuminated by consciousness.

The essential psychosynthesis view is that we are incarnations of the Self'. Our energy is embodied and made individual in that we are here in our bodies. We cannot deny the body without denying our very existence as 'little sparks of the spiritual Self'. And taking this to be the case, it is of vital importance to the work of psychosynthesis that we bring a sense of harmony and well-being into our bodies. We can only do this by including, not denying, the physical body with all its sensations.

EMOTIONAL ACCESS

We access our emotions through our bodies and every emotional experience is truly a body experience, not an intellectual one. There is a constant interaction between our bodies and our emotions. Try to imagine experiencing fear or anger without the body. How could adrenalin give us the energy to flee or fight without the body to do it with? Or try to imagine loving without a body. How could we truly express love without arms to hold someone?

For one reason or another, most of us have an excess of emotional energy held within our bodies. This can be released through cathartic techniques, many of which are used in psychosynthesis. When we discharge emotional energy through catharsis, however, it is important to remember we do not do this just for the sake of it, but rather we do it as part of the overall process of personal development. The basis of catharsis is simple. We live again, as realistically as we possibly can, events or situations from our past which created emotional disturbances within us. If we really relive these experiences to the fullest degree, we can now discharge the emotions that perhaps we could not discharge at the time. This way we release some of the emotional holding in our bodies and 'dissolve' some of our bodily armour. We can repeat the catharsis for any experience until it no longer holds an emotional charge and thus free ourselves from the imprisonment of this past episode.

If we just effect catharsis, however, without dealing with the causes behind the original trauma, then as with all 'dis-ease', the symptoms will return. We have to get to the root cause behind the problem, and this is where other psychosynthesis techniques, including visualisation, can be very effective. In fact in originally reliving the experience, we are using the imagination to re-create the visual, auditory and kinetic aspects of that time. It is clear, therefore, that it does not really matter whether what is remembered actually happened or not, just that the person reliving it believes this is what happened. For a full and effective cathartic release, the client must have a clear contact with the guide. This does not mean there has to be actual physical contact, but for the sense of well-being that comes after catharsis to last, the guide must be fully present physically, emotionally and mentally for the client.

When we deny our natural emotional need for experience and expression, and whenever we deny our natural instinctual impulses, we develop anxiety and neurosis. This is particu larly true for repressed sexual energy whether emotional or physical. If we repress this energy then we lose touch with our sensitivity. While this may mean we feel less pain when we are hurt, it also means we feel less pleasure when we are pleased. When we are repressed we experience tension and muscular contraction. Our bodies in this state can shrink, contract, and become fixed and rigidified. For our full psychosynthesis to be effective, we have to treat these conditions not only on the symbolic level of imagery, but also directly on the physical level. If we release repressed emotions and sensations directly through the body, we free a lot of energy. This allows us to be more alive, more real, more centred and connected on a transpersonal as well as a personal level. Indeed, it is with this free-flowing energy that we can truly experience the fullest, most manifest sense of the Self.

Through having a direct body experience, we can more readily access and, if we wish, change our emotional life, but it is true that we can only release the quantity of energy that we have built up in the first place. When the charge is high enough to get us deeply into the release of the energy, we may have a peak experience where we enter spiritual or 'transpersonal' realms. When this happens, we are contacting the Self through our bodies, and realising who we really are.

BEING HERE

When we try to incarnate fully into our physical bodies and express ourselves in the physical world, there are subpersonalities within us who do not want us to be really present in this way. Some subpersonalities appear to be in a state of not wanting to be incarnated, not wanting to be here on the planet. They take the line that it is difficult being alive, and it is far easier – and safer – to stay in an undifferentiated state. When we hear a voice within us say things like 'Why do I have to be here?', 'I'd rather kill myself' or 'I want my mummy' we can be fairly sure it is a part of us that fears coming into the world fully. Subpersonalities with such fears of incarnating can hold us back from being fully present and expressing our true purpose.

It is important that we consider all the ways that we avoid incarnating fully. We have to watch for 'yes but . . .' responses to things we could do which would manifest our purpose more clearly. We have to look for those times when we never quite make up our minds, when we avoid making decisions that would help us grow and develop and express ourselves in the world more clearly and more fully.

When we are in such states, one of the best ways to move forward and release some of the held-back energy is by expressing ourselves directly through our bodies. This might be through finding some underlying emotional blockage and expressing it in anger or sorrow, for instance. But often all we need to do is simply move – walk, dance, jump, run, it does not really matter – and the actual physical movement will bring us more clarity and help us make the decisions or take the actions we need.

Through physical work and the release of energy blockages in the body, we may express true transpersonal consciousness, a sense of the Self. It has been said that a new born baby is whole, complete in itself, and free from all restriction and fear. We can relive and truly feel in our bodies all that we knew and felt as babies. This can include the free flow of energy, a sense of connection to the Self and to the oneness of all life. Our bodies may be armoured, but when we start to release this armour, we find our bodies also carry all the knowledge and understanding we have of the transpersonal or spiritual realms. Our internal truths can be remembered, lived and relived through our bodies. We can appreciate this when, for example, we see a dancer who is no longer dancing but has become the dance. We can appreciate this most when we are the dancer ourselves.

If we believe there is a part of us that continues beyond our physical life, how much better to directly experience this in the body than just have it as a mental construct. Bodywork in psychosynthesis gives us the opportunity to master, channel and ground spiritual energies in our lives.

It is a basic mystical truth that there is nowhere to seek the Self except inside oneself. The true esoteric traditions stress this is a physical truth, not a metaphysical conception. Inside our bodies we can find the Self. Outside of ourselves we can only find otherness, not the Self, illusion not reality, glamour not truth. And when we find the Self inside ourselves, we tap into an endless source of creative energy which we can express easily and healthily not only through our bodies, but also our emotions, feelings and thoughts.

Another basic mystical truth is that the only time that exists is the present moment, everything is 'here and now'. After all, how can we be anywhere else but 'here' when if we move somewhere else, and someone asks us where we are, we answer that we are 'here'? And how can there be any other time than 'now' when at any and every moment the only time we can actually experience is this 'now'? We can remember yesterday or imagine tomorrow but can only experience this memory or fantasy in the present moment.

However we conceive of this 'here and now' experience, and whatever concepts we create around it, we can only really experience it in our bodies. When it is directly experienced it becomes a living expression of spiritual truth. To the person having such a transpersonal experience, time physically stops and space physically becomes alive and glowing with energy. Thus the true mystical experience is not something we think or feel, but something we live as a physical reality.

ENERGY CENTRES

Along with all the Eastern and Western methods for growth and development that include an understanding of the transpersonal, psychosynthesis utilises a knowledge of levels of energy in the body that are more subtle than just the physical ones. No one could deny the physical energy we have in our bodies, but once we start looking into ourselves we find there are other levels of energy within us, too. These 'subtle energies' have to be included in our work if we wish to achieve the fullest understanding of ourselves.

Of particular importance with this work is making a connection within our physical bodies to the energies that either help or hinder us from grounding. Many people who are drawn to spiritual work do not easily connect with their ground of being and often spend too much time with their 'head in the clouds'. A strong stable base is needed if we are going to start using the more subtle energies within our bodies. Psychosynthesis, in working with the body as well as in all its other techniques and methods, stresses the importance of clear, firm grounding.

Inside our bodies we have seven major energy centres or 'chakras'. Each of these chakras is a power centre within the body, involved with the experience and expression of energy particular to its individual function. They are all also totally interconnected and we really only describe them separately to help our understanding of them. Each chakra within our body may be either partially or fully closed or open. When a chakra is fully open it gives us powers of perception and creativity. The seven major body chakras are located at the base of the spine, the genitals, solar plexus, heart, throat, middle of the head, and at the top of the head.

Imagine what would happen if you were driving a car fairly fast when suddenly a large lorry pulls out in front of you. Most of us will feel a pain or a strong sensation of some kind in our solar plexus area. This is the contraction of the chakra located at that point. The solar plexus chakra has many functions, as have all the chakras. For instance, we can consciously radiate energy out from this area of our body. If we view someone as a 'bad' person in some way, for us they will be just that. On the other hand, if we radiate energy as light from our solar plexus, and start to see that same person in a positive way, then they are 'free' from the box we had previously put them in and are able to move on and change. We are also free too, for when we put someone in a box we restrict ourselves as much as we restrict them.

Imagine the sensation you sometimes have in your heart when someone you love is unhappy or sad. They might be said to 'pull at your heart strings'. This would be an experience of the heart chakra, which is very much connected with the experience and expression of love. On a deeper level, however, it is also involved with the balance between the energies of love and will, and for it to operate most effectively these energies have to be balanced. The heart is also associated with 'deeper' feelings and values such as service to others and altruism. In the current age, humanity as a whole is said to be moving towards a new connection and awakening of the heart values.

One aspect of chakra energy of particular interest is the dynamic between the three lowest chakras: the base of spine, sexual and solar plexus centres. Males often make a strong connection between the base of spine and sexual chakras, connecting power with sexuality. Women, on the other hand, tend to connect the base of spine centre more strongly with the solar plexus. Whether, in both cases, this is because of conditioning or genetics is not certain. It leads to confusion, however, when these centres are not properly functioning, and the energy required for the proper functioning of these three grounding energy centres is distorted. Because of these connections, there is a tendency for men to express their power distortions through their sexuality, whereas women tend to do so through their emotions. If we can distinguish between these energies and 'tease them apart' as it were, then they can be given the space to function properly on their own level. The interaction between them can then lead to a release of energy that helps clarify rather than cloud our personal issues regarding being here in the world, sexuality and power.

The diagram shows how the upper and lower chakras connect to each other and they all revolve around the heart, at the centre of the system. The heart, on this energy level, is equivalent to the personal self or 'I'. When our energies centre on the self through the heart in this way, there is connection between our different levels and the possibility that we can express ourselves on any level we wish in a clearly harmonious way. The diagram shows the condition achieved when the heart is truly open. The personality revolves around our central core identity, and the soul is clearly heard, seen

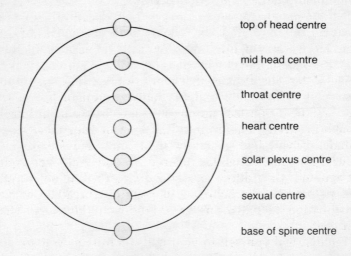

top of head centre

mid head centre

throat centre

heart centre

solar plexus centre

sexual centre

base of spine centre

The Circle of Energies

and felt in our lives. This is one of the major aims of psychosynthesis.

EXERCISE: A BODY OF SENSATION

Take a few deep breaths and start to become aware of any sensations you currently have in your body. Let your awareness focus on your body. Does it feel hot or cold? Are you heavy or light today? Where do you sense tensions and pain? Where do you feel loose and relaxed? Focus as clearly as you can on the sensations in your body. Use as many of your senses as you can to do this – can you hear your breath or your heartbeat? What do you see inside your body today? Do you feel there is too much or too little energy in any parts of your body?

As you become aware of each sensation that becomes foreground for you, bring your full attention to this sensation. Without becoming attached to it, look at what it is saying to you. Do you need to stretch or to move your body in some way? Observe all these sensations carefully, and honour their 'messages'. What do you need to do in your life to improve your relationship with your body?

Now expand your awareness to include all of your body. Become aware of your entire body and whether it is feeling cold or warm, tingling, alive or dull, in pain or pleasure. Allow yourself to feel your body. If you feel pain or tightness imagine, as you exhale, that you are breathing out through that part of the body and the tension or pain leaves with the breath. If you feel numb or 'dead' in any area, imagine you bring living energy into that area of your body as you inhale. If you feel generally tight and unaware, then let your in-breath bring you energy. If you feel over-excited or agitated, then allow excess energies to flow out through the palms of your hands with your out breath. Use your imagination to move energy around your body and 'heal' yourself.

Finally, feel yourself in your body as fully as you are able. Really be in your body. You might like to stamp your feet a few times to really feel the earth beneath you. Breathe in and out and be aware how your breathing roots you to earth. Decide to continue paying close attention to your body and to look after it in the coming days. Your body is your precious instrument of experience and expression, it is your temple in which you incarnate and choose to do your purpose in this life. Choose to treat such an important part of yourself with the respect it deserves.

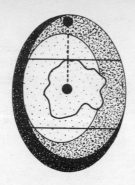

10 · LOVE AND CONNECTION

We are in continuous contact with each other, not only socially and on the physical plane, but also through the inter-penetrating currents of our thoughts and emotions . . . A sense of responsibility, understanding, compassion, love, and harmlessness are all links in the chain of right relationships which must be forged within our own hearts.

Roberto Assagioli

Psychosynthesis is not only involved with the individual, but also with groupings of people of all kinds. This encompasses our relationships with our parents, our children, our lovers and partners, our friends and colleagues and, on a wider level, all the groups to which we belong, including the whole of life. Psychosynthesis, understood as a natural process, encompasses all life and one of the main aims of psychosynthesis is to create 'right relationships' between all beings.

In this chapter we will look at some of the major aspects of interpersonal psychosynthesis, particularly as it relates to the individual and his or her primary relationships. The principles that we apply at this level, however, are the same ones we apply in psychosynthesis at other levels, suitably adapted. If we hold to the vision that we are not isolated but are part of one family of life, we are sharing in the vision of psychosynthesis.

95

When we filter this down through the different levels of relationships, we can still hold to the vision – one family of human beings through to the families into which we were born and which we have subsequently created with loved ones. The psychosynthesis family is an open family, one that encourages its member to find themselves and then express this knowledge and understanding in an attitude of loving awareness.

The psychosynthesis family is open to everyone for we are all interconnected on one level or another. The psychosynthesis family is inclusive rather than divisive, is strong rather than rigid, is caring but not smothering. All individuals are members of this family, and as soon as any individual starts consciously working on his or her own growth and evolution then that person is an active, giving member of this family.

At some times in our lives it is better to keep ourselves to ourselves and not share our energies. Psychosynthesis encourages us to respect our inner wisdom when such times occur in our lives, and not to think or feel guilty if we choose to be separate or alone. At other times we feel more like exploring who we are and what we do as it relates to other people (and other beings). Psychosynthesis offers a wealth of techniques and principles that can help us to facilitate this inner process. The very best way to explore our interpersonal expression, however, is quite simply through expressing ourselves. A good part of interpersonal relating is always trial and error and it is through taking risks and exploring this arena that we can truly learn and grow and play a more active part in our 'family'.

Sometimes we do not express ourselves at all as we would wish. Depending upon the reaction we receive, we may stop expressing altogether, suppress elements of our expression, or totally change direction. This applies not only to individual situations but to how we interact overall with other people. Some people are 'stopped altogether' most of the time and find it really hard to express themselves. Most of us suppress many different aspects of our inner world and do not express the totality of who we are. It is a major principle of interpersonal psychosynthesis that the first step to success is to accept ourselves for what we are. We learned the importance of acceptance in Chapter 8. Once we accept ourselves without judgement or censorship then we can simply express who we are without holding back. Then we open up the possibility of change both individually and interpersonally.

This does not mean we cannot or should not have secrets and, indeed, psychosynthesis respects the power of silence. Sometimes we share aspects of our growth and development too soon and thus dissipate some of the energy. Sometimes our 'need' to relate makes us share things more from a level of deficiency rather than inclusion. Our secret inner world needs to be cherished and fostered, and kept secret. Then, when we are choosing to be intimate we can allow others to share in some of this world, the power and awareness of which can be one of our major strengths.

The second major principle of interpersonal psychosynthesis is not to label people or 'put them in boxes'. If we want someone to stop seeing us in a certain way we have to stop seeing them that way. How often do we find ourselves saying something like 'you should be like me', or 'you should do what I do', instead of accepting the other person as he or she is? We can easily slip into seeing people in 'boxes'. We then start relating to the box instead of the person. Then we don't have to be really present or take any real risks in opening ourselves up, for once we put someone else in a box we put ourselves in a box too. Boxes are not noted for having great interpersonal relationships with one another! Fortunately, however, the opposite is also true: if we accept someone for what they are and do not label or box them, then we give them the space to treat us similarly.

Sometimes we rightly feel we should not be demanding, should give the other person more space, more love, or whatever. It is also important, however, to be aware of our own needs and openly express these too. So long as we can choose to accept the response to our demand, whether it be 'yes', 'no', or 'not for now', we are then entering into an active inter-relationship that allows both parties room to express and receive love. Also it is true that people tend to match our expectations. If we decide another person is going to say no then they will tend to do just that. We always get back what we put out – so the more we label someone else the more we become labelled ourselves. The more we expect of someone

97

the more is expected of us. And – luckily – the more we love someone and allow them to be themselves, the more we are loved and allowed to be ourselves.

When we acknowledge another person and honour their uniqueness and individuality, we set the scene for true love to emerge. We also open up the possibility of change, which is often why we find it so scary to do this. If things change we imagine we might lose out in some way so we cling tenaciously to what is, as if our lives depended upon it, and are even willing to risk the pain this may involve. When change occurs our lives do change. If we take the risk of letting others truly be themselves, though, then the likelihood is the change will be life-enhancing and positive. This is not always easy, of course, but at least through trying we can move ourselves forward in a positive direction. This leads us towards the third major principle of interpersonal psychosynthesis which is the understanding that to be loved, the only thing we have to give up is the experience of not being loved.

PROJECTION AND PERCEPTION

We have a tendency to project onto other people or the world in general all the ideas and images, fantasies, feelings and thoughts that we have about other people and the world. This projection can take place consciously or unconsciously. In this way, each of us creates our own reality, different, by the nature of this projection, from everyone else's reality. Thus, for instance, a dog to one person may be an emotional comfort, a trusted companion, whereas the same dog, to another person, may be a dangerous beast best avoided. Similarly, we may be angry about something another person has done and through projection see them as being angry at us. The energies that we project onto others then get attracted back to us, and we believe we were right all along.

It is of great importance that, wherever possible, we re-own all these projections and relate to people in a more direct way. One way of re-owning projection is to start honouring ourselves and trusting that what we feel is okay. We can then start to honour other people in a similar way. When we give ourselves the right to be, to grumble and moan if that's what we need to do, to be angry or loving, or whatever we need, then we create the space in which we can allow the same for others.

For any relationship to work to the fullest degree, the other person or people in it have to be willing to do the same. But it is a basic truth of any interpersonal relationship that it really does only take one person to change it. If we start acting in this way then we create change. We are not victims to other people or circumstances and always have the ability to change what we wish to change. Some of the best ways of creating such change include appreciating the differences between ourselves and other people, being willing to hear both the good and the bad people say about us, and giving people good feedback when they do things which clearly honour us for who we are. We can also treat any of the problems which arise between us and other people as blessings which give both us and them the opportunity to grow.

Basically we have to accept the other person for who they are, even if we cannot accept some aspects of their behaviour. There is a major difference between who someone is and what they do. Once we start relating to who they are then we are relating to them at a level of soul rather than personality. At this level all conflicts and disharmonies offer us the chance of growth. If we would like aspects of our relationship to be different then we cannot really blame anyone else but ourselves. Even if we could genuinely blame another, blaming someone is never a positive way forward, it just builds another barrier between us and them.

Of course, our personal reality is not just projection, there are many other components too. It has been said that our personal reality is primarily a combination of projection and perception. What we have to work with in any relationship is our perceptual reality. All we ever can do, really, is to work on our end of a relationship. We create and live by our own beliefs and actions. If we can learn to stop projecting our anger, sadness or whatever and start accepting it as ours, then we have taken a major step to improving our relationships, whether they be personal or of any other kind. We are then in a position where we can start seeing the other people involved for who they really are. We move then towards more of an 'I-Thou' relationship where we can express ourselves clearly and allow the clearer expression of the other person or people involved.

The first step has to be re-owning our projections, however. There is a simple technique for starting to do this. We start by recalling a difficult situation with another person and taking some time to really picture and feel this situation. Then we imagine ourselves as if we were actually the other person. We imagine ourselves seeing the situation from their viewpoint. After taking some time doing this, we imagine we toss the other person as we are seeing them a rope and, lassoing our projections, we slowly bring them back to the centre of our body. The more energy you put into feeling this is really happening, the more effective it is. We can choose to truly be ourselves and let others be themselves.

We cannot always deal with projections on our own however, and have to deal with the other person or people involved. One way of re-owning a projection is to express what we are feeling to the person directly (if we feel the relationship can take it). Simply by doing this we start to sort out the negativity between us. We have to find the underlying need that is not being fulfilled in the relationship, for example, the need for love or attention. If we see someone as angry, for instance, it is always worth checking out how angry we are – and then asking ourselves if we are expressing that emotion. Projection can often be spotted through the emotional charge it carries – we do not simply observe someone else is angry but we feel deeply affected. It is often rightly said that what we observe in someone else must also be in us or we wouldn't be able to recognise it.

THE PRIMARY SCENARIO

The 'primary scenario' for all our subsequent relationships is the one we experience in our families with our parents or guardians. It is useful if we can distinguish what actually happened in our primary relationships from what we imagine happened or simply believe without consideration. One way of doing this, discreetly if necessary, is to ask the other people involved how they view what happened. What your mother, for instance, saw happening in those early days of your relationship with her is no more 'the truth' than what you saw happening. But having different perspectives on the primary scenario can help us get a clearer, more complete picture.

We can also use our imagination and visualisation to help us re-create and learn from these early days. For instance, we can simply relax, close our eyes and allow a symbol to emerge that represents our primary family relationship. If we trust that the symbol which emerges is right for us at this time, and without judgement or censorship, simply allow such a symbol to appear in our mind's eye, then we can use this symbol to learn more about ourselves. If the symbol were a house on fire, for example, what might that tell us about the relationship? And, if the symbol was this, what could we do to change it? We might put the fire out perhaps, or allow the fire to run its course and then rebuild the house anew, but this time better than it ever was before.

We can also meditate upon our primary scenario and see what reflective and receptive meditation brings up for us (see chapter 5 for how to do this kind of meditation). We might, for instance, meditate upon the roles we played in our family. What skills did you learn from your family that are useful to you as an adult? What role models did you have in your family that aid you now? What roles did you play in your family that have meaning for you now (for example hero, peacemaker, troublemaker, joker, etc.)? Once we start finding the answers to these questions and consequently raising our consciousness in this way, we can then creatively find ways of changing not the actual family as it is now, or the events that 'actually' happened in the past, but our way of relating to this. We might even start to think of our families as chosen by us, and as having given us exactly what we needed.

The primary scenario forms the basis of all our future relating. Emotional patterns are transferred from parental relationships to personal ones. Perhaps our mothers or fathers exhibited over-development of their maternal or paternal roles, and were over protective. Perhaps, at the other extreme, they were over strict and restrictive. We can ask ourselves if we follow these patterns? Perhaps our parents were prone to do their living through their children – us. Are we repeating this pattern? Perhaps within us there is an over-development of romantic ideals. Perhaps we are obsessed by sex? Where did we get these ways of relating from?

We learn the ways we relate from our parents. If our relationship with them was clearly formed, then we know it is okay to be ourselves (to love ourselves) and it is okay to change (to empower ourselves). If these relationships were not so clearly defined, and in most of us this is exactly the case, then we exhibit corresponding distortions. We need to ask ourselves exactly what did our parents teach us about love and power? And we need to remember that we are not victims to some 'horrible ogres' whose conscious or unconscious aim was to cause us pain in later life. It is always true that, whatever we do, it is the best we can do at that time. This is equally true of other people, including our parents or guardians. Realising this brings acceptance, and true acceptance, as we have already learned, brings a clarity to our ability to be ourselves, and our ability to be both loving and wilful.

Just as we can bless any apparent obstacle to our growth and development, so we can bless our parents for doing the best they could. Forgiveness removes any lack of wholeness. Forgiveness brings love – both to the person forgiven and to the forgiver. We can never have enough forgiveness.

THE EXPRESSION OF LOVE

We can love ourselves or other people either from our sense of self, our centre, or in a more partial way, perhaps from a needy subpersonality. There is nothing wrong with loving someone in a partial way so long as we do not become identified with it in a way that does them or us a disservice. When we love from our centre we can be more objective, loving without attachment, caring but not overwhelming, strong but not manipulative.

To love from a subpersonality usually involves various aspects of need – I love you because you give me something or other. It depends upon the response – I won't love you any more unless you continue giving me whatever it is. To love from the self is to be proactive rather than reactive, to love someone for who and what they are rather than what they do, to be able to say I still love you despite what you are doing. Love from a subpersonality is usually shallower and more whimsical whereas love from the self is deeper and more lasting. Love from the centre is whole rather than partial, complete rather than fragmented. It is a synthesis of love and will, thinking, feeling and sensing. In this way it is complete and gives a sense of freedom rather than bondage.

We may try to understand love through analysing it in this way, but it is still love, however. Love quite simply just is. If it comes through a subpersonality it may be less whole, more needy, more reactive, but it is still love and we have the power within us to change it, to transform it into a more centred love. As we discussed in chapter 3, if we consciously work on meeting the needs of a part of us it can change and become more self-sufficient. When this happens, the love this subpersonality expresses can also become more self-sufficient. Parts of us that feel little or no love can have their 'love element' expanded whilst parts of us that have lots of love but express it in a distorted way can have their 'love element' refined. This is a basic principle for all psychosynthesis work, that we can elevate or expand energies we have too little of and refine or purify those energies of which we have too much.

When we realise and express love, we find its qualities abound. True love, of ourselves or others, gives us the energy for creative acts, it gives us insights and confidence, it strengthens and nourishes us, and, perhaps most importantly, it allows us to discover more about our true, inner selves. Often it is more difficult to realise and express self-love than it is to express love to others. Yet how much richer and more meaningful our lives become if we allow ourselves some self-love. This does not mean narcissistically becoming enamoured of our bodies, our emotions, feelings, thoughts or even our deepest soul connections. What it does mean is to accept ourselves for what we are, in totality. When we accept ourselves in this way we realise the greatest love within and are more able to express it.

Love in itself is often not enough, however, and it has to be coupled with understanding, otherwise it can blindly cause problems where it aims to release, can maim and spoil where it intends to free and encourage, can become sentimental instead of simply being itself. Love to be truly helpful has to be applied with wisdom and understanding.

If we see only our own view point and do not truly see the position of others, then we are obscuring the free flow of love. If we assert ourselves at the expense of others, in an artificial, excessive or inappropriate way, then we block love. If we have prejudices and preconceived ideas about how love should be expressed then we block love that way too. But if we let love be, let it flow through us as if we are channels for its greater energy, and if we work on making ourselves more conscious and more efficient channels for this energy, then love is our sustenance and salvation.

There is no such thing as an 'ideal relationship' but we can all consciously choose to create a reality in which we move towards rather than away from such a goal. In an ideal relationship we would relate in a holistic way. This would mean including all parts of our personality, dark as well as light. We would see the other person or people involved as equally whole and love them unconditionally. We would own our shadow, and not project it onto others. We would love without need or deficiency. We also would be willing to surrender to how the relationship evolves. We can move towards this ideal in all our relationships, but for it to become the primary focus we have to work at it, not because we think we should but because we really want to.

SEXUAL RELATING

To isolate sex in a relationship and try to understand it out of context is not very effective. We can understand sex better if we see it as part of a whole picture that includes all the other components of the relationship. It is very rare for sex to be a purely biological act, for it always involves feelings, emotions, thoughts, fantasies, all our resistances, our attachments, our fears and so on. Sex is often used in a relationship as means to a different end than the obvious one. It can be used to avoid problems, to avoid boredom, to overcome other difficulties in the relationship, to have power over the other person, and so on.

On the other hand, sex can be viewed as spiritual, as a holy act of union between people. When one and one come together sex does not give us two, it gives us a newly formed, ecstatic one again. Our inner desire for Unity can be met and fulfilled through a positive attitude towards sex. Books abound on sexual techniques, but the most important technique is in bringing awareness into our sexual lives. We can apply all the principles we learn for improving ourselves to improving our sexual relating. Awareness in sex brings vast amounts of energy for us to use in whatever way seems appropriate to us at the time. Used wisely, the energy of sex continues to increase, and can promote our successful psychosynthesis.

Most sexual problems fall into either or both of these categories: not operating sexually (too little), and only operating sexually (too much). As with anything of which we have too little or too much, we can apply the principles of elevation and refinement. When we explore our sexuality with a psychosynthesis guide we explore such questions as: What are the inner qualities behind the forms in which we relate sexually? Do we live out emotional patterns from the past in our sexuality? Are we attached to sex in such a way that our self-image is dependent upon our sexual relating? Are we able to both dis-identify from and identify with our sexuality when it is appropriate to do so? What meaning has sexuality for us? How has our attitude to sex been conditioned, especially in the primary scenario?

The exploration of our interpersonal expression, including sexuality, is perhaps the most exciting aspect of our existence in this life. It gives us the opportunity to know ourselves not only singly, as ourselves, but in combination with other people. We can extend our explorations to include all the beings on the planet earth, or we can focus on ourselves and our most intimate relationships. But however we explore our love and

105

connection we can come to realise both our uniqueness and our total interdependence.

EXERCISE: THE RELATIONSHIP WHEEL

Using a large piece of paper, draw a circle in the middle of it, quarter the rest of the space and put the names of four people with whom you are currently involved at the corners of the four boxes.

Using the circle at the middle as a focus, tune into your centre and clearly self-identify. Then choose one of the four people and do a free drawing in their 'box' to represent the relationship. Do not just draw a representation of the person, but tune into what the interaction between you feels like and try to represent this in your drawing. You can do this with a pencil, colours and as complicated or as simple as you wish; the important thing is to get down a representation of the current state of your relationship with this person.

When you are ready, tune back to your centre (the circle in the middle), then choose to go into another box and do a drawing for the relationship with that person. Repeat the process until you have a drawing in all four boxes.

When you have four drawings, spend some time tuning into your centre then look at the four relationships and see what

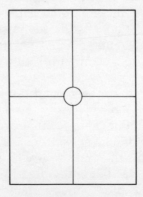

Four Relationships

differences you can find in the drawings, and what common elements there are. You can look for colour, shading, broken or unbroken lines, shapes and patterns as well as what is more obviously depicted in the actual shapes drawn. You might like to share this work with someone else, perhaps one or more of the people involved.

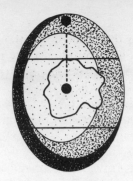

11 · THE SPIRIT OF SYNTHESIS

Let us feel and obey the urge aroused by the great need of healing the serious ills which at present are affecting humanity; let us realise the contribution we can make to the creation of a new civilization characterised by an harmonious integration and cooperation, pervaded by the spirit of synthesis.

Roberto Assagioli

Just as in the last chapter we saw that psychosynthesis comes alive and reaches some of its most meaningful insights when it is applied to relationships between individuals, we also find that psychosynthesis can have a vital part to play in the totality of interdependence between all living creatures. No one really exists as an isolated individual, anyway, for we all have involved and intimate relationships with other people and beings and our world in general, and thus we are truly interdependent. If we look at the whole of life in this way, we can see the potential, at least, for one family of living beings that co-exists harmoniously within itself and within the world it inhabits. On a spiritual level we can imagine the transpersonal Self as that which includes all the individual parts that make up the collective totality of existence and which is beyond each individual part. It is a general principle of psychosynthesis that the whole is greater than the sum of the parts.

If four people stand around a heavy object and they try to lift it into the air they may manage it, but there is a lot of effort involved and the whole procedure will appear clumsy and uncoordinated. If before they try to lift the weight they breathe together, matching their breathing to a common cycle, then they count from one to ten together and all lift at the same moment, they will find the weight is remarkably easy to lift. There is nothing mystical or magical about this. The four people trying to lift the object together but in an uncoordinated way are 'the sum of the parts'. Their lifting capacity is the sum of the lifting capacity of all four of them minus what they lose through not being synthesised into one 'lifing unit'. If they perform acts to bring their action together then they become a 'whole which is greater than the sum of the parts'. The lifting becomes easy, and, you will find if you try this with some friends, is accompanied by the release of much energy. What was an effort before is transformed into a pleasure.

We all make groups like this to perform our various tasks in life. These groups include our family, groups we form locally in our town for various purposes, our work groups, social classes, unions of various kinds, our national groups, and so on through the group we call the entire human family to the group that includes all living beings. If we can apply this principle of synthesis to all these groups to which we belong then we find that the tasks become easier and there is a release of positive energy which can be used not only for the good of the group involved but also for other associated groups as well.

It is rarely that simple, however. Problems arise between individuals within groups, and between groups, that are not dissimilar to the problems that arise within the individual. As we have already discussed, the individual personality is composed of many different subpersonalities, and the people in any group can be compared to subpersonalities. The methods and techniques used in psychosynthesis to harmonise the inner world can be equally well applied to the outer world. Indeed, the drive towards unity we feel inside when we touch into the deepest aspects of our nature can be seen and applied to outer groups and situations.

When we make this connection we start to realise that the Self creates diversity from unity in order that all beings can find their own way to realise the unity from whence they came and to which they are returning. We are divided for the sake of love, for in love we can find ourselves again and, in finding ourselves, discover that our separation was an illusion. We have the opportunity from this place of division to form a union, to come together with another being and be at one with him or her, or even to come together with all other beings and realise a total union. Without the division no such knowledge would be possible. Whilst we are in this illusion of duality, however, we can help bring more beauty and harmony into the world through our clear consciousness of loving what we do and doing what we love. Then we help move the whole of life towards that final goal, the supreme synthesis where all parts of life come together and realise the whole that includes all yet transcends each individual part.

It is important to stress that this is not an ungrounded, 'mystical' view of life or the place of individuals within the unfolding of the universe. Of course, no one would want to deny the reality of a mystical experience which separates an individual from their mundane, earthly existence and, in a state of bliss, leads them temporarily to forget all outer reality and the environment. If we become attached to such experiences, however, we fall into the mystical trap. Psychosynthesis stresses the importance of avoiding this through always paying attention to bringing all transpersonal energies back to ground and finding a way of expressing them in the 'ordinary world'.

The mystical experience should not be seen as an end in itself but rather a step along the way, from which the individual who has the fortune to have such an experience can draw creative energy, and enthusiasm. The true mystical experience also brings with it the desire to come back into the world to express the energies involved and help one's fellow human beings to experience this enlightenment. The 'mystic' who remains spaced out has 'missed the boat' that carries us all, irrespective of our experiences, towards the final goal of fully realised and consciously shared unity.

The other mystical trap is to believe that once one has reached some sort of blissful state, or received some sense of enlightenment, that this is all there is to it. It is the experience of all the great mystics that enlightenment is neither an end in itself nor, as such, does it last forever. Nothing remains the same, everything changes, and the enlightened state is no exception to this cosmic rule. Everything that is alive is in a constant state of movement, constantly renewing itself as it moves from moment to moment. If you stop moving, quite simply you die (and even then this is an illusion for in death we may find at the very least decay and a return to an energy state and perhaps more). Each revelation has to be grounded and expressed. In psychosynthesis we see the true mystic as the one who is working to express the energies with which he or she has connected, not the one who remains connected and has nothing left to say, do or feel.

THE PRINCIPLE OF SYNTHESIS

It is worth stressing the principle of synthesis: that the whole is greater than the sum of the parts. If we look at a painting and analyse it into its component parts we may find the different colours, brush strokes, shading and light, figures and background, we may even find beautiful scenes depicted within it, trees, people, places . . . but we have to see it as a whole, in its entirety before we can realise the value of it as a great work of art. What comes out of that synthesised whole is something beyond any or all of the individual components, perhaps something that even transcends the artist's original conception.

In the psychological application of this principle of synthesis, we stress the importance of each part being made whole in itself before it can be truly synthesised with other parts. If one of your subpersonalities is not 'whole', if it has wants at odds with your true purpose, if it has unheard and unmet needs, if its true qualities are obscured, then how can it take its true place as part of the whole personality without creating disharmony? It is so important, therefore, that we do not short change our work on the personality, which is, after all, the 'vessel' through which we express our innermost spiritual truths.

Synthesis is, in fact, an organic process. We cannot force it or make it happen, but what we can do is co-operate with and facilitate the process as it unfolds organically. One way of achieving a move towards actualising the potential that we all have is to work at balancing and synthesising the opposites that exist within us. If you are a man then you can work at bringing out the 'female' within you to create more harmony and balance. If you are an idealist then perhaps you need some practicality to help balance your personality. If you are attached to the spiritual path then perhaps a little sensuality may lighten your load. Each of us as individuals has our own inner connection, our own inner world of opposites. The work of synthesis, in this area, is to find these opposites within ourselves so we can balance them and create a clearer synthesis.

If for example, you were very at ease with your intellectual powers, at home in the mental world, you may want to make more connection to your feelings. If your mental side then, was, say, the size of a football and your feelings the size of a tennis ball, the technique of synthesis would *not* be to make the mental connection smaller until it was the size of the 'tennis ball feelings'. The opposite would be the case, to elevate your feelings until they match the size of your mental attributes. At the same time you could be refining this mental side to make it, in itself, clearer and more harmonious. The work of synthesis involves, therefore, a continuous process of elevation of the smaller element of any pair of opposites and the refinement of the more developed polarity.

A further principle of synthesis is that we can never solve a problem at its own level. If we take the example of two subpersonalities who are in disagreement, perhaps about whether we should take a certain decision in life, then so long as we remain on the level of their argument it will continue. Both the parts are fighting for their rights, even for their very survival. Each part knows what is best for us and is going to 'damn-well' make sure we do just that. If we can gain a perspective from a different level, however, we may be able to find a way to overcome the difficulty. One part of you wants to go out right now and another part wants to stay in. From a third place of greater perspective we might find that a compromise can be reached – you'll stay in now but go out later, for example.

Once we have dis-identified from both of the parts in this way, we have moved ourselves, if not actually to the place of the Self, at least to a clearer space. We are no longer caught in the problem at its own level. Once we are thus placed, we can then start looking for a synthesis, perhaps through asking ourselves what it would be like if the two parts not only found a compromise but actually came together. We can do this at least partly through not being too attached to fulfilling the individual wants of each part but looking towards finding out what their real needs are. When we do this we are moving these parts a little towards unity, towards the synthesising centre that is the Self.

Such a synthesis is not only possible, it is desirable. We can be both loving and strong, intuitive and logical, spontaneous and disciplined, idealistic and practical, spiritual and sensual and so on. Indeed, what we usually find is that when we start bringing opposites together we again get a whole that is greater than the sum of the parts. A new reality is created. I am still loving but now I can be strong when it is necessary and not allow people to walk all over me, taking advantage of my good nature. I can still be a spiritual person and indeed can express my connection to the transpersonal better, not in spite of but because of my new connection to the world of the senses.

When we create synthesis in our lives, when parts within us come together into a new relationship, or when we find a way of moving closer to someone or something else in this true synthesising manner, then we not only grow as individuals, we add to the total growth of all sentient beings. We also free energy that was previously blocked and involved in conflict, energy we can then put to creative uses. The more we move towards our personal synthesis, the closer we move the whole of creation towards the time when there is a universal synthesis.

COLLECTIVE RESPONSIBILITY

Everything we do in our lives makes a difference not only to ourselves but to everyone and everything else. Until fairly recently in human history it would have seemed unthinkable, in moral as well as practical terms, to imagine that even the collective totality of humankind could make an appreciable difference to our home planet. Yet now we realise that everything we do not only makes a difference, but those things we do carelessly and selfishly can put the lives of all the creatures on this planet in jeopardy. We have evolved into 'planetary people' and to fully honour this growth we have to take responsibility for our individual actions and the actions of our race as a whole. Everything we do can make an enormous difference, from that single squirt of an aerosol spray to closing our eyes and ears to the plight of many of our fellow human beings, let alone the even sorrier plight of many of the other species of life on this planet who have an equal right to be here.

Both our knowledge about what is happening in the world around us – with its wars, disease, disharmony and ecological imbalance – and a sense of inner inadequacy can make us believe that there is nothing we as individuals can do to change the world in any way. When we connect with our innermost nature, with a sense of Self, however, we find we are also connected to everyone and everything else. We are part of a collective consciousness that is totally inclusive and infinitely caring. Realising we are a part of this collective shows us that everything we do *does* make a difference.

Some of the more spiritual connections we make in psychosynthesis work can help us realise that all life forms, not just human beings, are part of a totally interconnected and inseparable energy field. While most of us may spend a large part of our lives imagining that we are separate and disconnected, once we start to explore the deeper aspects of our being we discover the underlying truth of our connection. We may not be able to 'be there' all the time, indeed it may not be right for us to stay in such a state, but once we have the intimation of its real existence, once we actually experience it in ourselves, there is no looking back. We have 'set our sights' on the clarity and connection that comes from such realisations and we try to make each move we take a step in that direction.

When we realise that we are connected to everyone and everything else, we start to have a different perspective on time and space. In reality we are no less connected to an ant on a distant island in the South Pacific than we are to our noses! While it may be very rare for us humans to realise this connection, we can start moving our awareness in that direction. We can start to cultivate within ourselves a sense of this 'global consciousness'. We can realise our individual consciousness is a small but significant piece of the total consciousness of life on our planet.

Many of the exercises and techniques used in psychosynthesis can help us have an inkling of this awareness and, perhaps more importantly, can ground this awareness in our everyday lives. When we ground this awareness it helps us take actions that move the total collective consciousness forward in its positive evolutionary path. It is not an exaggeration to say that one small act made by one individual at one moment in time can make a profound difference. When we care for others, both those immediately within our field of awareness and activity, but also all living and non-living things generally, we are grounding this consciousness. When we care for our environment, both locally and generally, we are also grounding this consciousness. Every conscious act we make that includes such caring furthers the cause of global awareness in this way. We can find many different ways to contribute to this cause and each way adds to the richness of our experience. Perhaps such awareness will bring about some cures for the ills which currently threaten not only our individual existence but the existence of life as we know it on our planet.

SOMEWHERE IN TIME

At school many of us were given a misleading view of evolution. We were either told directly, or it was suggested to us indirectly, that the human being is the apotheosis or pinnacle of evolution. Everything that had come before was designed simply to lead to the human race and, in creating us, evolution had fulfilled its task. The evolutionary process could be condensed into a twenty-four hour day. In this model, life appears a little before noon and the whole of human history takes place in the last five minutes before midnight. This interesting but false description of evolution suggests we are somehow 'the end'. Quite what is meant to happen when midnight strikes is not described.

A better model is created if we map the sun's expected lifespan onto the twenty-four hour day. This lifespan is currently estimated at around twenty billion years. In this model, the time is now around eight o'clock in the morning and the whole of life has been around for just the last couple of seconds. Human existence so far amounts, therefore, to a split second around eight in the morning. Seen in this light our perspective on evolution changes.

It would be possible to take this second model of the evolutionary process and say: why bother then? If we are such a small, insignificant moment in the time of our planet, even if we destroy ourselves and all life with us, it's only a couple of seconds out of a whole day. The planet will survive and go on without us, and if we're lucky it may even get round to giving us another chance!

On the other hand, why not bother? Look out of your window and see a piece of the beautiful blue sky, listen to the sounds of birds simply singing in a wood, touch one hand against another and feel the wonder of life, present in your every moment. Why not bother – after all, we've come this far in a couple of seconds, let's see what we can make of the next hour or two.

EXERCISE: THE INNER GUIDE

Relax and centre yourself in the usual way. Imagine you are in a meadow where the sun is shining and the birds are singing. Spend some time really feeling your presence in this meadow. Notice what you can hear, what you can see, what you feel.

At one edge of the meadow is a path leading up to the top of a nearby hill. Start to walk in that direction, really feeling your feet on the ground beneath you. Start an ascent up the hill, taking your time to thoroughly enjoy the sights and sensations you experience on your journey.

As you reach the top of the hill become aware that you are about to meet someone who is intimately involved with the evolution of your life. This person is your inner guide – you might see him or her as a wise old person, as a guardian angel, or simply as someone whose eyes express great love and care for you. However you visualise this person, let the image of him or her appear clearly before you. Allow yourself to experience fully the excitement and interest such a contact invokes.

You can now engage this being in a dialogue and, in whatever way seems best to you at this time, ask about any issues, questions, choices or problems you currently have in your life. The dialogue may be verbal or non verbal, it may take place on a visual or symbolic level, but however it occurs really relish this time you are spending with your inner guide.

Also ask about global awareness and the state of our planet and what you can be doing to help the current precarious situation. Let your inner guide's wisdom and understanding help you realise your connection, your ability to love and your power to cause change to occur.

When you are ready, thank your guide for having appeared to you and, returning back down the hill, enter the meadow and once more feel your feet firmly placed on the ground. Bring your consciousness back to your room and spend some time considering what you have learned and how you can put this learning into practice in your life.

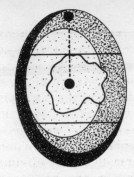

AFTERWORD

Psychosynthesis is not a doctrine or a 'school' of psychology ... There is no orthodoxy in psychosynthesis and no one, beginning with myself, should be considered its exclusive representative or leader. Each of its exponents tries to express and apply it as well as he or she is able to, and all who read or listen to its message, or receive the benefit of the use of the methods of psychosynthesis can decide how successful any exponent has been or will be in expressing its 'spirit'.

Roberto Assagioli

Sometimes it is said that psychosynthesis is 'a psychology that includes the transpersonal or spiritual'. For me it is more than that — if I had to describe it in this way I'd rather say it is 'a method of spiritual realisation that includes psychology'. Many people use psychosynthesis for counselling or personal therapy and find it very effective. Others use it for enhancing their creative work and do not feel the need to include the spiritual realms, and for them this is most effective. Psychosynthesis is a unique method, however, in that it centres on the Self around which all else is said to cluster or revolve. When we centre on the Self in this way we are making a commitment to spiritual unfolding as well as to psychological development. Instead of being 'a personality that includes the self we become 'the Self which *has* a personality'.

It is also sometimes said that psychosynthesis is 'something beyond analysis'. Yet how can we truly separate analysis and synthesis when to synthesise something you have to have analysed it first? Roberto Assagioli stressed the importance of a thorough knowledge of the personality as the first step in the psychosynthesis process. He said that an extensive exploration of the unconscious has to be taken first before the process of psychosynthesis can move on to the realisation of the Self as the central truth of the individual. This exploration explicitly includes entering the depths of the unconscious, the traditional aim of psychoanalysis. So psychosynthesis is not 'beyond analysis' but rather includes it.

I've also heard it said that psychosynthesis is 'too much about the light and it denies the dark'. This could be true of some psychosynthesis practitioners, but it is not true of psychosynthesis itself. The map of consciousness used in psychosynthesis gives equal weight to the dark, 'lower' unconscious as it does to the light 'higher' unconscious. Psychosynthesis work that does not involve the exciting challenge of including the 'shadow' side of our being is probably not very interesting and definitely partial.

It is very exciting to live within the vision and by the principles of psychosynthesis. How we do this creates our own version of psychosynthesis. If we want to share it with others, we have to honour our personal vision of what it is and equally honour their 'version' of it too. We also have to remember that we are all teachers. Psychosynthesis is best understood and applied when it is an equally shared experience. In this book I have shared with you the elements of psychosynthesis and some of my personal excitement at having such a useful method for use in my life. If you are inspired to do more psychosynthesis after reading this book, then appendix 2 includes some suggestions of what you can do next. Remember, however, that you already know the best psychosynthesis guide there is, and he or she is that same guide that knows you best, too – your own inner wisdom and understanding.

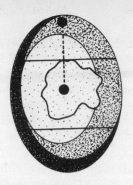

Appendix 1 ·
Psychosynthesis
Users

During the period when I was writing this book, I sent out question-naires to graduates of the English psychosynthesis centres, asking them how they were applying psychosynthesis in their work. I feel the following selection of responses speak for themselves, and clearly show how psychosynthesis can be applied successfully in numerous different fields. The list here is not, of course, exhaustive, and psychosynthesis can be used by an individual in any work situation. In most areas where psychosynthesis is applied, some techniques are of more use than others. Often the most relevant use of psychosynthesis is with the person's own process rather in the actual work itself. At the very least, however, by personally applying the principles and practices of psychosynthesis, the individual will be contributing to the harmony and well-being of the other people with whom they come into contact.

Social Work

'In my job as a residential social worker I use the more direct interventions of psychosynthesis, but have little use for visualisation. I feel I am much more aware of my needs, strengths and weaknesses. I can come from a much more aware position in a variety of interpersonal relationships than before.'

'If I am finding a particular client difficult to work with, I sometimes use imagery to understand the process evoked in me by the client. When I can find some way of understanding and dealing with what is happening in me, I can better deal with it in the client. I also quite often use the exercise in dis-identification, again for myself, to give me more perspective. I find psychosynthesis more helpful in a diagnostic sense than therapeutically, but I find then one has to work with the therapeutic relationship, help the client "work through" the issues.'

'Psychosynthesis relates to my ideas about the brotherhood of man. Humanity is one family. It is difficult sometimes to relate these ideas to my present work which tends to be with those families in the most difficult circumstances where political and economic factors become more pressing, but I can hold the vision whilst I work.'

Medicine

'I keep the egg diagram in mind even if I am not overtly using psychosynthesis. I am aware that the patient in front of me is more than his or her problems. As I work in a NHS psychiatric clinic, I usually do not discuss concepts such as "higher self" with patients and there is no need to unless people ask me questions and want to know more.'

'Growth, healing and transformation are a grace that may follow on the willingness to experience the pain of limitation. Conversely, trying to change or avoid the pain prevents growth.'

'I use it everyday, by finding the I-Thou in every relationship, which is very hard at times. It allows me to work in a more real, direct and worthwhile way with the dying and grieving. I use the meditative techniques as teaching aids and attempt to mobilise my patients' choices. I find that connecting with the patient's transpersonal experience deepens and broadens the relationship I have with them. Subpersonality work is particularly rewarding as patients connect with this idea instantly.'

'I have learned through psychosynthesis to care for myself a great deal better than I used to. I have learned I have needs too, which is quite a discovery for an obsessional, professional carer.'

Business

'I run training courses for local government organisations. These courses usually concern interpersonal skills, service delivery, supervisory and management skills, and I have found the application of psychosynthesis principles fundamental not only to what I teach, but to how I teach it. For example, when teaching the "basics of good communication" I stress the importance of accepting the other person, even if you reject what they say, think or do; that the essential person exists apart from, and is more important than, their words, thoughts or actions, which are much more ephemeral. In the same spirit I accept and value everybody participating in my courses, even if I feel saddened, angered or frightened by their behaviour or words.'

'My work broadened out into training programmes on counselling, team work, assertiveness, stress and very importantly the training of trainers. Also I work a lot with the "change process" in organisations. In some ways psychosynthesis leads to more problems than solutions. The insights gained add more joy but more depression too. It opens up roads that cannot be turned back. It has made me a more resilient person, able to ride the waves more easily. On the other hand, my frustration with the world out there has become more total. If I had to name one thing, it has given me a sense of community with people who can share a common-enough language.'

'Work is a place we create in order to grow. It is as much a growth point as many one-to-one relationships or crises. Psychosynthesis helps in making it OK to express fear, destructive feelings. conflicts, confusion, inconsistency, doubts, low self esteem, which are all otherwise unacceptable things to express in the business environment.'

Parenthood

Being a parent is undoubtedly a full time occupation (even if we are doing other work at the same time!). The quotes here give an indication of how interpersonal psychosynthesis is applied in the parent-child relationship, but they apply to other 'work' relationships just as well.

'Psychosynthesis is with me without my "using" it. However I did use it during the delivery of my son last year. I had a very long labour of twenty-five hours. At various stages I used visualisation, dis-identification and my will to bring my son into the visible world.'

'In my relationship with myself and others, especially my two teenage children, I remember that they are "souls" and "personalities" in their own right. I attempt to help them to express themselves even when I don't find it easy.'

'Psychosynthesis is a psychology and philosophy for living, it is fundamental to my life. It helps me deal with the notion of life as a journey, and how the individual and collective are empowered and brought into right relationship is vitally enacted in the family situation.'

Teaching

'At a personal level it empowers me to express and operate more successfully and effectively. At a deeper level, it enables me to stay in touch with who I am. To work more through my intuition and to experience my life as a traveller on a path with many other selves, who may really be me. Using psychosynthesis in the classroom, I experimented initially with various techniques and this was successful both from the point of view of the children's response and the academic work it stimulated. I worked with feelings, encouraging each child to express them through painting, written work and talking . . . I also use reflective meditation and visualisation to help develop concentration and observation, getting the class to visualise numbers, shapes, objects and complete pictures. I use reflective meditation in a much less focused version: choosing a quality such as "cooperation", the class write it down and then they spend ten minutes writing words and phrases that come into their minds. I direct the process by bringing their attention to each of the senses, for example, what colour is cooperation? what sounds or music remind you of cooperation?'

'In my polytechnic teaching, psychosynthesis has been a useful tool for taking some of the stress away around my relationship to superiors and colleagues. It has to some extent been helpful in altering that fundamental basis of education, the relationship that we have with students, to one demonstrating less of an imbalance of power. I do not see psychosynthesis as a science. It is a poetic vision. I make no effort to apply it, in the same way I do not apply Shakespeare, though both inform me of what it is to be a human being more than the psychology in our universities.'

'One particular way in which change takes place lies in a greater capacity and willingness to accept nastiness – in other people, in myself and in events; this does not mean "accepting" in the sense of liking or approving but in understanding there is an ultimate purpose and value behind the "bad" as well as the "good".'

Counselling

'Psychosynthesis in the last analysis is about life. If it is not lived in life then what is the point of working with it? Psychosynthesis is nothing, out of relationship, except a series of maps and models. Its great contribution has been through applying it experientially, giving it context and meaning.'

'Psychosynthesis is a way of seeing and of remembering the wholeness from which we have separated ourselves. It is a psychology that includes the dark depths of our being as well as the spiritual heights. The spiritual path alone can lack both substance and rootedness, and psychology alone lacks vision and meaning. Psychosynthesis speaks to the inner journey. Cancer is one of the greatest challenges facing us in the world today; how do we come to terms with such a mysterious disease? How do we explore a mystery? It is not just an individual's disease, it takes place in a family context and points to a threshold that society itself is facing.'

'I use psychosynthesis in my work as a counsellor to help people see the choices that are open to them in their everyday lives and how marginal changes in their behaviour can widen their horizons.'

Administration

'Psychosynthesis is not applied directly in my paid work, but it is one of a number of approaches that help to make sense of things and give tools for decisions and handling issues.'

'At present I do computer administration work so I do not apply psychosynthesis as a psychotherapist would do. However it has given me an awareness of group, team, and individual dynamics and enables me to be more tolerant and understanding and assertive when I need to be. I also have to train people occasionally and have a better intuition about peoples' learning patterns than I would have had before.'

'As a person in my late fifties, I find as I review my life there is a tendency to regret the apparently missed opportunities. Psychosynthesis has helped me see the value in the path I have trodden and also to make fuller use of my life's experience rather than to devalue what I have been.'

Art

'In my art workshops I focus on the creative process more than the product. It is engaging with the material world and investing it with a person's imagination and vision. It strengthens the senses other than words and can give a new perspective on life. I handle the material as well as the structure of the courses through my psychosynthesis spectacles and will talk of harmonising aspects of self and working in contrasting media as different subpersonalities might. I use the guided imagery of journeys, and work with painting through obstacles by viewing the obstacle from different perspectives.'

'As a writer, the value of inclusiveness and an awareness of what is beyond my self or my subject is enormous. The principle that I am part of a greater whole and I must fulfil a purpose by taking my place in that whole is a sustaining life principle for me. From it come qualities of acceptance and a willingness not always to know. Having struggled and tried so hard to know, I give in and trust and suddenly the way becomes clear.'

'Psychosynthesis gives me enjoyment and fun in learning and developing. Weaknesses are stepping stones for growth and development.'

Healing

'I work by getting an image of the pain and finding out what it is saying. Sometimes it is enough to learn simply to acknowledge and include the offending painful part, instead of cursing it.'

'I see no division between my life and my work. Gradually the psychological wholeness and healing which is my understanding of psychosynthesis means that I am responsible for lack of harmony and destruction. There is a choice to perpetuate this situation or to live my life and work through my truth, evoking and initiating wholeness and healing.'

Astrology

'Astrological psychosynthesis uses the birth chart as a tool to explore an individual's potential. It is a path to greater self-awareness and so provides an opportunity for living a fuller life, in harmony with the energy of the environment. The birth chart can provide valuable clues to subpersonalities, how they interact with one another, which ones shout loudest and which are underdeveloped as a result of childhood conditioning.'

'I was trained in astrology and I certainly apply the theory and practice of subpersonalities, for example, polarities such as mystic and pragmatist, love and will. Transits indicate the kind of transpersonal or personal energies that want to be integrated.'

Therapy

'Mostly I think the application of psychosynthesis in my work is subtle and subliminal! I am often aware of the triangle that psychosynthesis presents so well – the third place or level which is somewhere other than, and more than, the sum of the polarities being explored. I envisage psychosynthesis as a kind of building block in my discovery of my inner resources . . . so it is now an integral part of who I am and my experience.'

'Psychosynthesis has encouraged me to learn how to begin to know and accept myself as I am. This has enabled periodic moments of contact with my own deep personal integrity which admits and accepts my dark and distorted side. These excruciatingly painful moments have born the fruits of the spirit: compassion, understanding and lightness of heart. Also the insight that the "burning bush" is not out there in the wilderness but within my own heart, so that the voice which says "I am that I am" resonates within myself when I fall silent and listen.'

'As well as working as a psychosynthesis guide I also run groups. The psychosynthesis model is flexible enough to be useful in all the group work I do. The techniques are simple and practical and allow for the wisdom of each individual to be the real guide. We cannot grow as human beings whilst continuing to ignore the fact that we pollute our nest, destroy the oceans or rain forests and that species are becoming extinct at an alarming rate. We do not exist in isolation. Growth in a purely human context is meaningless.'

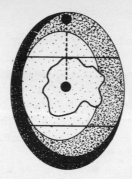

APPENDIX 2 · WHERE DO YOU GO FROM HERE?

Psychosynthesis may be started from various points and angles at the same time, and the different methods and activities can be wisely alternated . . . according to circumstances and inner conditions.

Roberto Assagioli

After reading this book you may feel that you would like to use psychosynthesis in one or a combination of three basic ways:
(1) to foster your individual growth and development;
(2) to add new skills to and develop your work in whatever field that may be;
(3) to become a psychosynthesis guide, therapist or counsellor.

Assagioli stressed the 'central decisive importance of the human factor, of a living interpersonal relation' between the psychosynthesis guide and the client. If you desire to pursue psychosynthesis further, then I would stress that, whatever your reasons for wanting this, the most vital factor will be your personal psychosynthesis sessions. Nothing can replace the experience and growth possible through one-to-one sessions.

It may be the case for you, however, that the time is not right for you to work individually with a psychosynthesis guide. The following, therefore, are suggestions of what you can do to increase your knowledge, understanding and, most importantly, experience of psychosynthesis work. None of these suggestions need to be taken singly and, in fact, are probably best approached in the various combinations and at the appropriate times that suit your own personal evolution.

Individual study: a lot can be gleaned from reading books on psychosynthesis and related subjects, particularly those books which offer you practical suggestions and exercises, for reading is best accompanied by experiences so that you connect what you read with your own personal process.

Individual therapy and counselling: as stressed above, this is the most important and fruitful way to learn about psychosynthesis, for through individual sessions you learn through your own, personal connections. A stipulation of all good psychosynthesis training courses would be that the trainee pursues a course of individual psychosynthesis therapy.

Talks and presentations: most of the psychosynthesis centres and institutes will either have occasional public presentations on psychosynthesis or will be able to tell you of such events. Many individual psychosynthesis practitioners also give talks and presentations that centre on psychosynthesis, often as it is applied in their work or life generally.

Group therapy and seminars: most psychosynthesis centres and institutes have a 'public programme' which will include various workshops and seminars either directly on psychosynthesis or on particular aspects and applications. Many individual practitioners of psychosynthesis also run such groups, either directly on psychosynthesis or applying psychosynthesis to other areas of work and interest.

The author of this book is available for individual sessions, group presentations, workshops and seminars on psychosynthesis and various related subjects. He can be contacted through the publisher.

Training courses: as well as one-off introductory weekends, most of the psychosynthesis centres and institutes run a 'fundamentals' or 'essentials' of psychosynthesis course, often part time over a matter of a few months, which introduces participants to the principles and practices of psychosynthesis. These introductory training courses are very popular and contain enough material for anyone to use psychosynthesis in their own work and life in an informed and practical way. Beyond this, many centres also have more long term, in-depth training programmes which often lead to a certificate of qualification for psychosynthesis counselling and therapy.

Whichever of these options may attract you, the next step will probably be for you to contact either a local psychosynthesis centre or to look locally for advertisements and notices about events and individual practitioners in your area. May your search for inner wisdom and understanding be fruitful, and may you come to a self-realisation that nurtures both your own individual experience and expression and that of the planet as a whole.

PSYCHOSYNTHESIS CENTRES & INSTITUTES

Listed below are Centres and Institutes where professional training, courses for the general public, and individual psychosynthesis counselling or therapy may be arranged. I would advise you to request details from more than one centre and decide from the information you receive which one attracts you the most. The addresses given are currently correct, but of course the older this book is when you read it, the more likely it will be that some of them may have changed.

For individual psychosynthesis therapy or counselling, an alternative to contacting a centre is to look in local listings and information boards in your area. There are individual psychosynthesis practitioners in most areas who not only see individual clients but also run workshops and courses. Before embarking on individual work, ask the guide about his or her training, but also remember that your individual discrimination and sense about the person are ultimately the best criteria on which to base a decision. If it does not work out to your satisfaction do not be afraid to voice your concerns and be willing to change if necessary.

U.K.

The Psychosynthesis & Education Trust
48–50 Guildford Road, London SW8 2BU
(071) 622 8295
[Professional Training & Programme of Short Courses]

Re-Vision – Psychosynthesis Vision in Practice
8 Chatsworth Road, London NW2 4BN
(081) 451 2165
[Professional Training & Self Development]

The Psychosynthesis Institute
The Barn, Nans Park Lane, London NW7 4HH
(081) 959 2330
[Professional Training]

U.S.A.

There are one or more psychosynthesis centres in many states, and it would be impossible to list them all here. The same advice applies as above. You may be able to get a directory of centres, or advice on local practitioners from:

The Psychosynthesis Directory
Sacramento Psychosynthesis Centre
P.O. Box 161572, Sacramento, California 95816
[This Directory currently lists centres in the following states: California, Colorado, Florida, Kentucky, Maine, Massachusetts, Minnesota, Missouri, New Hampshire, New Mexico, New York, Ohio, Pennsylvania, Vermont, Virginia, Washington]

The following are just a selection of psychosynthesis centres. They may be willing to supply further information about your specific area.

Australia

Psychosynthesis Centre
P.O. Box 43, Bondi Junction, New South Wales 2022

Canada

Psychosynthesis Pathways of Montreal
4816 Hutchinson, Outremont, Montreal, Quebec H2V 4A3

Ireland

Institute of Psychosynthesis
19 Clyde Road, Dublin 4

Italy

Instituto Di Psiosintesi
Via San Domenico 16, 50133 Firenze

The Netherlands

Centrum Voor Psychosynthese
Postbus 85156, 3508 AD Utrecht

New Zealand

Institute of Psychosynthesis
7 Farnol Street, Aukland 2

Portugal

Palmoinho Centre De Psicossintesse
Serra do Louro (4 Moinho), 2950 Palmela

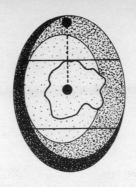

FURTHER READING

Books

Assagioli, Roberto *Psychosynthesis* Turnstone, 1975 (A manual of principles and techniques)

Assagioli, Roberto *The Act of Will* Wildwood House, 1974 (The nature of the will, and the stages of willing)

Eastcott, Michal *'I' The Story of The Self* Rider, 1979 (Exploring consciousness from a largely psychosynthesis perspective)

Ferrucci, Piero *What We May Be* Turnstone, 1982 (The visions and techniques of psychosynthesis)

Hardy, Jean *A Psychology With A Soul* Arkana, 1987 (Psychosynthesis in an evolutionary context)

Whitmore, Diana *Psychosynthesis In Education: The Joy of Learning* Turnstone, 1986 (Psychosynthesis applied to educational theory and practice)

Articles

Many psychosynthesis institutes have copies of articles and papers by Roberto Assagioli and other practitioners available for sale. Some of the quotes at the beginning of chapters in this book come from such material. If you are interested, contact your nearest centre.

INDEX

133